1,001
Kitchen
Tips & Tricks

1,001 Kitchen
Tips & Tricks

Helpful Hints for Cooking, Baking, and Cleaning

Mary Rose Quigg

Skyhorse Publishing

Skyhorse Publishing books may be purchased in bulk at special discounts for sales promotion, corporate gifts, fund-raising, or educational purposes. Special editions can also be created to specifications. For details, contact the Special Sales Department, Skyhorse Publishing, 307 West 36th Street, 11th Floor, New York, NY 10018 or info@skyhorsepublishing.com.

Skyhorse® and Skyhorse Publishing® are registered trademarks of Skyhorse Publishing, Inc.®, a Delaware corporation.

Visit our website at www.skyhorsepublishing.com.

10 9 8 7 6 5 4 3 2 1

Library of Congress Cataloging-in-Publication Data is available on file.

Cover design by David Ter-Avanesyan
Cover images by Shutterstock

Print ISBN: 978-1-5107-6228-2
Ebook ISBN: 978-1-5107-7285-4

Printed in China

Contents

Acknowledgments

I am grateful to all the family for their encouragement when I was compiling this book. Special word of thanks to Joe and Karen for their proofreading and helpful comments.

Introduction

The kitchen is known as the "hub" of any house. With this in mind, this compilation of hints will assist with its smooth running.

Natural products are used wherever appropriate to encourage an environmentally friendly workplace.

The range of hints covers the care of kitchen appliances, utensils, and cooking equipment that should help to extend their life span. The cooking section gives helpful tips on meat, fish, and dairy products as well as invaluable baking advice.

The poems and proverbs included should give some food for thought or just sheer amusement. I have enjoyed compiling this collection of hints and hope you find the book interesting and advantageous.

—Mary Rose

Kitchen Appliances

CHOOSING KITCHEN APPLIANCES

Select the thickest counter worktop you can afford. Laminated counters tend to have greater resistance to heat and damage. Some materials are easier to clean and maintain than others. Bleach or fruit juice spills need to be removed immediately from laminates and wood, but stains or burns on solid surface materials can be gently scrubbed away. Granite is particularly easy to care for, while wood may need regular oiling. Scratches on stainless steel are self-healing and the material is naturally hygienic.

. . . .

Before purchasing new appliances, decide if they are to be built into cabinets or free-standing. Look at ways to make appliances more accessible. For example, raise the dishwasher so that less bending is required.

. . . .

A sink can be a focal point of the kitchen or just functional depending on its design. Stainless steel sinks are hygienic and coordinate with most other appliances. Choose the sink design that is most practical and ensure that your largest pan can fit into the main bowl.

. . . .

Choose a dishwasher that does not have an intrusive noise level. It must also be energy efficient and economic with water consumption.

. . . .

Convection ovens give the best distribution of temperature. Decide on the style you require. Ease of cleaning is essential.

. . . .

Decide if a fridge/freezer or separate refrigerator and freezer is the most beneficial for the household. Check the energy rating, the defrosting method, adjustable shelf height, and the strength of the door shelves.

. . . .

A separate home freezer can be convenient but it takes good food management to make it really pay for itself. Generally a chest-style freezer costs less to run than an upright model.

REFRIGERATOR & FREEZER

Do not put the refrigerator directly beside a heat source or in a sunny position in the kitchen. Do not cover the top and allow air to circulate around the outside of the unit. Make sure the unit is level.

. . . .

Unplug the refrigerator or freezer and pull out 3–4 times a year to clean underneath. Use a vacuum to remove dust from front coils and motor to keep it operating efficiently.

. . . .

To reach under the refrigerator or radiator, staple a small sponge to the end of a yardstick.

. . . .

Clean the door gaskets only with baking soda; bleach or harsh detergents will deteriorate them.

. . . .

Check for adequate tightness of the insulating seam around the door by placing a lit flashlight inside the refrigerator at nighttime and closing the door. Turn off the lights in the room and see if any light escapes from the seams. This will help pinpoint any leaks.

. . . .

Put a piece of paper in the door and close it firmly. If the door is sealed properly it should take a hard tug to remove the paper. To help seal the door, put a thin layer of petroleum jelly on the gasket.

. . . .

To prevent grease buildup on top of the refrigerator, after cleaning buff some paste wax into the surface.

. . . .

Remove odors from a refrigerator by either placing a vanilla extract-soaked cotton ball, charcoal, coffee grounds, baking soda, or a slice of lemon in it at all times.

. . . .

Frequent opening of the refrigerator door allows cooled air to escape. Note the temperature in the unit. The optimum temperature for a refrigerator is 35°–38°F.

. . . .

Combine 1 gallon (5 liters) hot water, 1 cup clear ammonia, ½ cup vinegar, and ¼ cup baking soda. Pour into a spray bottle or use from a bowl with a sponge. This no-rinse formula is a degreaser that prevents mold and mildew. Wipe down the entire refrigerator with this solution, including the drawers and shelves.

. . . .

Line the ice-making compartment of a refrigerator with a sheet of aluminum foil and the ice cube trays will not stick.

. . . .

When freezing foods, use a freezer wrap that is air-, vapor-, and moisture-proof, such as freezer bags, aluminum foil, or airtight containers. Force out as much air as possible from bags or containers and be sure they are tightly sealed. Trapped air can cause the food to dry out, change color, and develop an off-flavor called freezer burn.

. . . .

When loading a freezer, avoid adding too much warm food into the freezer at one time. This slows the rate of freezing and can raise the temperature of already frozen foods. The result is lower food quality. As a general rule, no more than 3 pounds (1.2 kilograms) food per cubic foot of freezer space should be added in a 24-hour period. Put packages in the coldest part of the freezer first (against the walls or bottom of the compartment). Leave space between packages so cold air can circulate. Label and date freezer foods.

. . . .

Avoid storing hard-to-freeze items such as ice cream or orange juice on the freezer door shelves.

. . . . .

Fill empty spaces in the freezer with plastic boxes or jars filled with water; a freezer runs more economically when the contents are closely packed. Defrost regularly.

. . . . .

Some foods including potatoes (unless mashed), citrus fruits, mayonnaise, cream fillings, cream, cooked egg whites, gelatin salads, and sour cream cannot be frozen successfully without deteriorating.

. . . . .

The safest way to thaw foods is to place them in the refrigerator. For faster thawing, put frozen packages in a watertight plastic bag and place them in a sink of cold water. Change the water often to slow bacterial growth on the outer layers while the inner areas thaw. Foods can also be safely defrosted in a microwave but should be cooked immediately after thawing.

. . . . .

Do not thaw perishable foods at room temperature as this can cause bacteria to grow rapidly.

. . . . .

When defrosting a freezer, wrap the frozen food in newspaper until the task is completed.

. . . . .

Line the bottom of a chest freezer with a clean white sheet. When it is time to defrost, it acts as a giant towel and makes cleaning much easier.

. . . .

To help speed up defrosting a freezer, use a fan directed toward the frost to loosen it. Or place pots of boiling water in the freezer, close the lid, and leave for 20 minutes. Do not use sharp implements to remove frost as they can puncture the freezer. Wash the inside with a warm water solution of mild detergent or baking soda, rinse and wipe dry. Vacuum dust off condenser coils.

. . . .

When going on vacation, place a few ice cubes in a plastic bag in the freezer. If a power failure occurs while away and the food thaws and then refreezes you will know from the bag of cubes.

. . . .

Ordinary masking tape makes great freezer tape; it can be written on and peels off easily.

. . . .

Put a paper towel in with baked goods when freezing them. The paper absorbs the moisture and prevents freezer burns.

. . . .

When freezing liquids leave ½ inch (1.2 centimeters) headspace at the top of the container to allow for expansion.

. . . .

Do not freeze cabbage, lettuce or other raw leafy greens, cucumbers, celery, or radishes—they will be mushy when thawed.

· · · ·

Do not put hot or warm food in the refrigerator as it can cause the temperature to rise inside the unit.

· · · ·

Cut a complete strip from the top of frozen food bags and use as a tie when returning the bag to the freezer.

· · · ·

Wrapping the outside of ice cream containers in aluminum foil will help prevent freezer burn.

Soft ice cream can become hard after some of it has been consumed. Put a freezer bag into the space to prevent this happening.

. . . . .

Unstick stuck stamps or photographs by placing them in the freezer for 10–20 minutes. Gently break apart using a butter knife. Put back into freezer if they do not come apart easily.

. . . . .

Use automatic-dishwasher detergent to clean refrigerators, stoves, floors, walls, and glass. Dissolve ¼ cup powder in 1 gallon (5 liters) of very hot water. Wipe with a dry cloth. Wear rubber gloves and test area first for colorfastness.

STOVES, OVENS & GRILLS

To unclog burners on a gas stove, boil them in a solution of 4 ounces (100 grams) baking soda and 4 pints (2.4 liters) water.

. . . .

Keep solid electric hotplates clean by brushing them with a stiff brush.

. . . .

Soak removable stovetop parts for 15 minutes in a solution of 3 pints (1.8 liters) hot water and 2 teaspoons each of washing powder and soda crystals. Wash down the rest of the stove with the solution. Wear rubber gloves.

. . . .

To clean white enamel stoves, combine 1 tablespoon paraffin and 2 tablespoons salt. Rub onto burn stains with a piece of flannel. Then wash well with hot water and baking soda.

· · · ·

While the oven is warm, wet any spills and sprinkle with salt. Scrape off when the oven cools and wash as usual.

· · · ·

Or combine 2 tablespoons liquid soap and 2 teaspoons borax in a spray bottle and top off with warm water. Spray the mixture directly on the burned-on food and leave to soak for 20 minutes. Scour with steel wool to remove.

· · · ·

Clean the inside of an oven window by dampening a cloth, then dipping it into a small bowl of baking soda and scrubbing in a circular motion.

· · · ·

Heat oven to 200°F/100°C, then turn off the oven and place a shallow glass bowl containing ½ cup ammonia on the top shelf. Put a large pan of boiling water on the bottom shelf. Close the oven and leave overnight. Open the oven door and air for a while before washing off with soap and water. Even the hard baked-on grease will wash off easily.

· · · ·

Spread a paste of baking soda and water on oven racks and place them between layers of wet newspaper. Spray water generously over the bottom of the oven then cover the grime generously with baking soda. Spray more water over the top. Leave overnight. Wipe out the loosened debris with an old rag or paper towels. Remove the residue with liquid detergent on a damp sponge. Remove the paper from the racks and rinse well.

· · · ·

To get rid of unpleasant or chemical oven-cleaner odors in an oven, heat it to 350°F/180°C, place an ovenproof bowl with water and lemon juice or orange peel in the oven and leave for 30 minutes. Turn off heat and leave until cool.

· · · ·

To clean a glass oven door, apply a paste of biological washing powder and water and leave for 2 hours then wipe off.

· · · ·

When the clean cycle is completed in a self-cleaning oven, take out the racks and rub them with a wadded-up piece of wax paper and they will be easier to slide in and out.

· · · ·

Line the oven floor with heavy-duty aluminum foil. When the foil gets dirty, discard. Make sure vents are not covered with foil as the temperature could be distorted.

· · · ·

Toss salt on a grease fire on the stove or in the oven to smother flames. Never use water; it will only spatter the burning grease.

· · · ·

If a gas oven or stove has a pilot light, make sure the flame is blue and cone-shaped. A yellow "jumping" flame indicates the light is burning inefficiently.

. . . . .

To avoid getting the oven dirty, make sure casserole dishes are not overfilled. Put pies inside a large cake pan or on a baking sheet and make a foil tent over roasting meat.

. . . . .

Anchor ramekins in a hot water bath or bain-marie by placing them on a folded dishtowel. This prevents them moving around when lifting the dish in and out of the oven.

. . . . .

Clean the range hood filter by soaking it overnight in a pan of water with a dryer sheet. Scrub it clean. Or mix a thin paste of white vinegar and cream of tartar and spread it over the filter. Leave for 30 minutes and then scrub clean. Or run the filter through the full cycle in the dishwasher to remove any built-up grease. Repeat if necessary.

. . . . .

A handful of salt thrown on flames from meat dripping in barbecue grills will reduce the flames and deaden the smoke without cooling the coals as water does.

. . . . .

To spruce up the outside of a barbecue, while it is still warm, rub with a cloth soaked with cooking oil. Before storing, oil the burner to help reduce rusting.

. . . . .

To avoid the base of a charcoal barbecue wearing through, pour 1 inch (2.5 centimeters) sand over the base for the coals to sit on.

. . . . .

To clean the rack of a grill, spray window cleaner on the grill while it is still warm. It will be much easier to clean. Or wrap wet newspaper around the grill to help soften the carbonized food stains. Or leave the racks lying on grass overnight and they will be easily cleaned in the morning.

. . . . .

When an uncleaned grill is needed urgently, turn the empty grill on to high, then, before use, rub the rack with a wire brush to remove the buildup of burned food easily.

DISHWASHER

Large chunks of food should be scraped off dishes before putting them in the dishwasher. Place dishes on the bottom rack with the soiled side facing toward the sprayer. Place baking sheets and platters near the sides and spoons and forks should be sorted in opposite directions.

. . . . .

Silver cutlery can be washed in the dishwasher, but not with stainless steel pieces. Stainless steel will damage real silver.

. . . . .

Place glassware, plastic items, and mugs on the prongs of the top rack to help keep them in place. Do not position them above the sprayer or close to the element.

. . . .

Put small objects in mesh bags to keep them from being scattered in the dishwasher.

. . . .

Opaque or decorated glasses should not be put in the dishwasher as they may turn yellow. Avoid putting sharp knives in the dishwasher as they may dull. Do not wash pewter or gold items as they may become discolored.

. . . .

Only run a dishwasher when it is full. When adding dishes, sprinkle a handful of baking soda on them and the bottom of the dishwasher to absorb odors.

. . . .

Make dishwasher soap by mixing equal parts baking soda and borax and use 2 tablespoons per load. Increase proportion of soda for hard water. Use vinegar in the rinse cycle.

. . . .

Turn off the heat dry cycle of the dishwasher. After the wash cycle, open the door and leave dishes to air dry.

. . . .

To clean the inside of a dishwasher, fill both soap cups full of vinegar and let it run through a full wash cycle. Or freshen it by adding a cupful of baking soda and running the machine through the rinse cycle only.

. . . .

Never use regular liquid hand soap in the dishwasher as it can cause a soapy disaster.

. . . .

If the water ports become clogged, use a pipe cleaner to clear the holes. Scrub filter screens with a stiff brush.

. . . .

Rid the kitchen sponge of germs by running it through the dishwasher.

. . . .

Since the dishwasher normally connects at the kitchen sink, turn the kitchen sink hot water on until hot water is at temperature peak. This will give a hot water start, saving heating power, and will help dissolve the powdered soap granules.

SINKS

A dripping tap can be fixed by opening the tap and pouring oil down the handle. The oil swells the washer and forms a better seal.

. . . .

To clean stains from sinks, line bottom with paper towels and pour on bleach. Leave for 30 minutes, then wipe clean.

. . . .

To remove water spots from stainless steel sinks, wipe with rubbing alcohol or white vinegar.

. . . .

To stop water from leaking out of the kitchen sink while doing dishes, put a piece of cling film between the drain and the drain stopper.

. . . .

Take a couple of pieces of bread, wad them into a ball, and use as an emergency sink stopper.

. . . .

Clear the sink drain by dropping three Alka-Seltzer tablets down the drain followed by a cup of white vinegar. Wait a few minutes, then run the hot water.

. . . .

Pour strong salt brine down the kitchen sink drain regularly to eliminate odors and keep grease from building up.

. . . .

Unblock sinks with soda crystals and hot water or baking powder followed by vinegar.

. . . .

"Fear less, hope more, eat less, chew more,
Whine less, breathe more, talk less, say more,
Hate less, love more, and all good things will be yours."
—Unknown

Rub rust marks on stainless steel sinks with lighter fluid, then wipe with regular kitchen cleaner.

. . . . .

Hair has a tendency to accumulate around bathroom sinks. Most products have difficulty picking up hair, as static electricity makes it cling to the porcelain. Moisten a paper towel and scrub the porcelain. The water will destroy the static charge, and the paper towel will be able to pick up all the hair. Do not flush away the towel as it could clog the plumbing system.

. . . . .

To disguise scratches on a stainless steel sink, rub with chrome polish, wipe off with a damp sponge, and shine thoroughly. Repeat if necessary.

SMALL APPLIANCES

Store little used appliances in cupboards to reduce clutter on the countertop.

. . . . .

Keep the mixing bowl from slipping on the countertop by putting a rubber mat or a damp cloth underneath it.

. . . . .

Avoid long, uninterrupted use of a blender. Such misuse can overheat the motor and possibly cause a breakdown.

. . . . .

Use glycerine or mineral oil to lubricate the movable parts of blenders or other kitchen appliances. Salad oil may corrode the metal, but mineral oil is noncorrosive. For easier cleaning, spray disks with vegetable oil before use.

. . . . .

When choosing a blender, metal bases are more durable and keep the appliance steadier when it is in use. Blenders with glass jars are heavier and generally more stable.

. . . . .

To clean a blender, add a little dishwashing liquid and half fill with hot tap water and blend. Add ice to sharpen blades, repeat if necessary. Use an old toothbrush or a cotton swab to clean between the small buttons on a blender.

If the blender is leaving black marks on a kitchen counter, glue soft plastic medicine bottle caps onto the feet.

. . . .

To remove a melted plastic bread wrapper from a toaster or coffeepot, rub petroleum jelly on the area, reheat the appliance, and use a paper towel to rub off the plastic. Nail polish remover will also remove the plastic but test first to make sure it does not remove the finish.

. . . .

Before cleaning a toaster oven, let it cool and use a nylon scrubber to clean the racks. The outside can be cleaned with a gentle abrasive or baking soda on a sponge. Clean the plastic sides with liquid dishwashing soap or a paste of baking soda and water.

. . . .

Clean out the crumb tray of a toaster oven often because it can be a fire hazard. Unplug the toaster first and use a handheld vacuum to remove crumbs. Or open the crumb tray on the base and hold the toaster over the sink or trash can and shake gently. Use a pipe cleaner or thin nylon brush to remove crumbs. Do not immerse the toaster in water.

. . . .

To stop waffles from sticking to the grid of the waffle iron, wash the grids with warm, soapy water. Rub the burned-on spots with a nylon scrubber and season the grids by rubbing or brushing them with vegetable oil. Wipe off any excess oil.

. . . .

Use rice to clean a coffee grinder and sharpen the blades.

· · · ·

To clean a burnt coffee-pot, heat the pot, add salt and ice, and swirl it around. Rinse thoroughly.

· · · ·

Keep a coffee-maker clean and fresh by adding ¼ cup baking soda to 1 cup of warm water and let it drip through. Then drip a pot of plain water through to rinse.

· · · ·

To remove the stale smell of coffee from a travel mug or flask, add 1 tablespoon dry rice to the flask, shake for a few minutes, and rinse well. Or stuff it with newspaper and leave for a few days.

· · · ·

To remove bitterness from percolators and coffeepots, fill with water, add 4 tablespoons salt, and percolate or boil as usual.

· · · ·

Remove stains and mineral deposits from a teapot by filling it with water and adding 1 tablespoon lemon juice and 2 tablespoons baking soda. Simmer for 15 minutes. Rinse and repeat if needed.

· · · ·

To clean a stainless steel teapot, add a denture-cleaning tablet to the pot and top it up with warm water. Leave for 1–2 hours and rinse well.

· · · ·

For lime deposit in a kettle, pour in 1 pint (600 milliliters) vinegar and top up with water, boil until lime is dissolved, rinse well. Or pour a can of cola into the kettle, boil, and rinse well. Descale kettles regularly.

. . . . .

Store and keep appliance cords neat by placing them in the inner cardboard tube from a used kitchen roll. Write details of the relevant appliance on the cardboard tube.

. . . . .

Before cleaning a meat grinder, run a piece of bread through it.

. . . . .

Pad a meat grinder or mincer clamp with a piece of plastic foam to make it grip tightly and not mark the worktop.

. . . . .

To avoid lime water spots on stainless steel, rub with a small amount of baby oil on a paper towel.

. . . . .

Shine stainless steel by rubbing with lemon juice or vinegar.

Microwaves

Never turn on an empty microwave as it can damage the unit.

. . . . .

Cooking times vary according to the wattage of an oven. Follow the instruction guide carefully. Use the lowest cooking time specified in a recipe as food dries out easily.

. . . . .

To gauge the energy output of a microwave, fill a glass measuring cup with exactly 1 cup tap water. Microwave, uncovered, on "high" until water begins to boil.

· · · · ·

If boiling occurs in wattage is:

Less than 3 minutes	600 to 700
3 to 4 minutes	500 to 600
More than 4 minutes	less than 500 watts

· · · · ·

Use only microwave safe dishes. If unsure about a dish, fill it half full of water, set it in the microwave and turn on the high power for 1 minute. If the dish gets hot, it is not safe for cooking. If the dish gets warm, it can be used for reheating, usually done at about 80 percent power. If the dish stays at room temperature, it is safe for all cooking.

· · · · ·

Round dishes heat food more evenly. The square corners on a dish receive more energy and the food in those corners will overcook.

· · · · ·

Arrange evenly sized food in a circle for more uniform cooking. Place thicker foods toward outer edges for faster cooking. Stir at least once during the cooking cycle.

· · · · ·

If a microwave does not have a liner, put a microwave-safe plate or paper towel underneath the food.

· · · · ·

When a recipe calls for foods to be elevated and there is no rack in the microwave, use an upside-down glass dish.

· · · ·

Food cooked in glass cookware can be viewed throughout cooking. Always use a dish twice the size of the contents to be cooked to avoid the food spilling out. Do not use gold or silver trimmed dishes. They could ruin the microwave.

· · · ·

Always reheat cooked food on half power in the microwave; this ensures the food reheats evenly without overcooking the edges while leaving the center cold.

· · · ·

Allow ample standing time after removing a dish from the microwave oven so that the heat will be distributed evenly throughout the food. Test for doneness after standing time.

· · · ·

When defrosting in the microwave leave about 2 inches (5 centimeters) between the food and the inside surface of the microwave to allow heat to circulate. Smaller items will defrost more evenly than larger pieces of food.

· · · ·

Decrease the liquid in a conventional recipe by one-fourth when converting it for the microwave.

· · · ·

Be careful of steam when cooking in the microwave.

· · · ·

Do not use the microwave for deep-frying, canning, or heating baby bottles. These applications do not allow adequate temperature control for safe results.

. . . .

Do not use a microwave oven if an object is caught in the door or if the door does not close firmly or is otherwise damaged. Keep the door and oven cavity edges clean. Do not use abrasives such as scouring pads.

. . . .

To clean spills in the microwave, cover them with a damp paper towel and turn the oven on high for 10 seconds. The mess wipes up easily as the oven cools. Stains in a microwave can be removed by rubbing the area with baking soda on a warm damp cloth.

. . . .

Remove microwave odors by adding 2 tablespoons baking soda or lemon juice to warm water in a glass bowl. Boil for 3 minutes and leave for a further 30 minutes. Remove the bowl and wipe oven clean with paper towels.

. . . .

Stay with the oven when cooking popcorn as heat buildup can cause a fire. Time heating per instructions, but veer toward the shorter time. To remove burnt popcorn smells from a microwave, boil ½ cup water and 1 teaspoon vanilla extract in a small bowl in the microwave. Leave overnight before wiping out.

. . . .

If heating water in a microwave, place a wooden stir stick or teabag in the cup to diffuse the energy. A much safer choice is to boil the water in a tea kettle.

. . . .

Use paper plates or coffee filters to cover food and avoid splatters in the microwave.

. . . .

Place damp paper towels over the food to be cooked in a microwave. The dampness holds the towel in place making a secure cover and the moisture helps the cooking process.

. . . .

When finished cooking use the towel to wipe down the inside of the microwave.

. . . .

Do not put paper bags or any other packaging materials in a microwave oven unless they are clearly marked microwave-safe. Some bags have metal fragments that could ignite.

. . . .

The microwave works best with foods that have high moisture content, like vegetables, fish, poultry, and fruits. Vegetables retain their natural fresh color and texture when cooked in the microwave.

MICROWAVE TIPS FOR SPECIFIC FOODS

Even if a microwave oven is not used to prepare an entire recipe, it is a time-saving convenience. Use it to shorten some of the preliminary chores in a recipe, such as melting butter or chocolate, toasting nuts or coconut, plumping dried fruit, or softening cream cheese.

Apples, Potatoes, Eggplant, and Squash—pierce before cooking to let off steam and avoid splattering.

Bacon—to easily separate, microwave for 35 seconds at full power.

Butter—to soften butter, heat at 50% power for 45 seconds.

Bread—when reheating rolls in the microwave always cover them with a cloth.

Chocolate block—melt at 100% power for 45 seconds per 1 ounce (25 grams) of chocolate.

Coconut—to toast a cup of coconut, spread out thinly on a plate and cook at full power for 2–3 minutes.

Cream and Eggs—cook at low power to avoid curdling.

Citrus Fruits—microwave for 20 seconds to get more juice when squeezed.

Crackers, Cereal, Cookies, or Potato Chips—freshen from stale by heating for 10–20 seconds at full power.

Egg—never cook a whole egg in its shell as it will explode.

Fish (frozen)—thaw in original container at 30% power.

Fruit (dried)—plump by putting in bowl with a little water and cooking at high power for 20 seconds.

Herbs—add during the standing time. Dry fresh herbs in the microwave.

Ice Cream—soften hard ice cream at 30% power for 20 seconds.

Onions—to peel onions more easily, place them in a covered container and microwave for 1-2 minutes at 100% power. This helps remove the "hot" flavor when served uncooked.

Salt—do not add until cooking is finished. Salt draws out moisture.

Sugar (brown)—to loosen hard packed sugar, place an apple slice in the bag and microwave at 100% for 5 seconds.

Vegetables—cook on high power for 6-7 minutes per 1 pound (450 grams). Add butter to the water before cooking. Cook in beef, chicken, or vegetable broth for better flavor. Cover dark green vegetables with wax paper for better color.

Useful Utensils

DISHES

For burned-on stains in baking dishes sprinkle baking soda over them and add white vinegar until the stains are covered. Allow to sit overnight, then clean as usual.

. . . .

To aid in washing dishes, add 1 tablespoon baking soda to the soapy water; it softens hands and cuts through grease.

. . . .

Sprinkle salt on greasy dishes to make them easier to clean. Salt will remove burned marks from the edges of pie dishes, stains on china or earthenware, and egg stains from cutlery.

. . . .

To clean glass cookware, first soak in a vinegar solution before washing as usual.

. . . .

Burned food can be removed from a glass baking dish by spraying it with oven cleaner and leaving it to soak for 30 minutes. The burned-on residue will be easier to wipe off.

. . . .

To make a slight crack in a dish disappear, mix 1⅓ cups nonfat dry milk with 3¾ cups water. Place the dish in a pan, cover with the milk solution, bring to a boil, and simmer for 45 minutes. In most cases, the crack will vanish.

. . . .

"Glass, china and reputation are easily cracked, but never well mended."
—Unknown

For cracks in fine porcelain, squeeze out a cotton wool pad in warm water and dip it in baking soda. Cover the area and leave for a few days, wetting the pad occasionally.

. . . .

Cut the nylon mesh bags from vegetables into several pieces and use as plastic scouring pads to clean dishes.

. . . .

Clean yellowing ovenproof dishes by soaking overnight in 5 pints (3 liters) warm water with ¼ pint (150 milliliters) bleach added.

. . . .

When storing fine china, put a paper plate between each plate to stop them from getting scratched when stacked.

Rub a small chip in a dish with an emery board or some fine sandpaper until it is smooth.

. . . .

When plastic wrap will not stick when covering a dish, moisten the outer edge of the dish before wrapping it.

. . . .

Use bleach to remove pencil-like marks on dinnerware caused by using stainless utensils. Or if the score has not penetrated the glaze use a pencil eraser.

. . . .

Never put sharp knives into soapy dishwater where they cannot be seen. Laundry detergents or automatic dishwasher detergents should not be used for hand washing dishes.

POTS & PANS

When buying pots and frying pans, ensure that they fit the burners on the stove. If larger or smaller than the burner, they will waste electricity or gas.

. . . .

Use flat-bottomed cookware on an electric range of a size that just covers the heat element. Slope-sided cookware is for cooking on gas.

. . . .

Pots and frying pans should be relatively heavy in weight. The metal should be of a good thickness. If they are light to lift, the metal used is too thin and will not absorb heat well.

. . . .

A good pot or pan usually has a layer of copper sandwiched between the metals in the bottom of the pan. Painted-on designs of grids and patterns in copper do not conduct heat.

. . . .

Keep the drip pans under the burners clean to reflect the heat back up to the pot. Dark-colored drip pans absorb heat and reduce the efficiency of the burner.

. . . .

Do not tap or hit the stirring ladle on the rim of the utensil to loosen foods that are stuck on the ladle. This repeated action, over time, tends to bend the rim out of shape and the matching lid will never give a tight fit.

. . . .

When finished using a pot or pan never place it in cold water, nor under cold running water. Drastic temperature changes will warp the utensil and if repeated over time, they will warp and no longer rest flat on the burner. Allow it to cool down on a heat resistant surface before washing.

. . . .

Never heat an empty pot or pan longer than 3–4 minutes.

. . . .

When storing pots and frying pans, hang them from their handles or stack them. If stacking nonstick pots and pans, place a clean rag between them to prevent the interiors from being scratched.

. . . .

"An unwatched pot boils immediately."
—H. F. Ellis

Avoid using sharp-edged ladles and large spoons to stir foods; even if they are made of plastic or wood they can easily scratch the nonstick surface, just as metal does.

· · · ·

For nonstick utensils, gently wipe out any remaining debris immediately after cooking, using a paper towel. Dried hard debris can scratch the nonstick surface when it is being rubbed off; if repeated regularly it can ruin the coating.

· · · ·

Cookware with nonstick coatings should not be heated dry for more than 30 seconds. Add the cooking fat before this because the nonstick coatings will degrade if heated dry for too long.

· · · ·

Remove stains from nonstick pans by sprinkling the surface with baking soda. Place lemon slices over the soda in a single layer. Add enough water to just cover the lemon and simmer until the stain diminishes. For stubborn stains remove from heat and allow pan to soak overnight.

· · · ·

To resmooth Teflon pans, boil 1 cup water, 2 tablespoons baking soda, and ½ cup liquid bleach in the pan for 5–10 minutes. Pour off and wash in soapy water, then rinse thoroughly. Before using, wipe the surface with salad oil.

· · · ·

Avoid steel-wool pads for cleaning pots. They can ruin a non-stick surface. Soak pots in water and liquid dishwashing soap then clean with a nylon pad.

. . . .

To clean the corners of pans cut up an old credit card and use as a plastic scraper.

. . . .

Frying pans with plastic handles can only be used on a stovetop and not in the oven, unless the label states that the handle is heat resistant up to a certain temperature.

. . . .

Metal lids are preferable to glass. Steam forms underneath the glass lid during cooking and the lid becomes cloudy.

. . . .

Flat-surfaced pans are much easier to scrape using a flat wooden spoon. Foods get caught in ridged surfaces.

. . . .

To prevent the base of a copper pot from staining, rub it circularly with a thick slice of lemon dipped in salt.

Use the leftover juice from a jar of dill pickles to clean the copper bottoms of pans. Pour juice in a large bowl and set the pan in it for 15 minutes. Or rub with tomato paste, scrub, and rinse.

· · · · ·

Remove stains on copper pans by salting the area and scouring with a cloth soaked in vinegar.

· · · · ·

Put lids on saucepans, unless a recipe states otherwise, and the food will cook more quickly.

· · · · ·

Soak pans that have held starchy food with cold water.

· · · · ·

To make pans easier to clean, remove the grease from them immediately after cooking by adding salt and wiping them with a paper towel. Or rub used teabags around the pan to break up the grease.

· · · · ·

Pour ¼ cup vinegar and some liquid dish soap into hot water and use to clean stainless steel pans. Do not use abrasives.

· · · · ·

Remove burned or baked food on pots or pans by putting a squirt of dishwasher detergent with water in the pan and leave for 20 minutes. Or add a few drops of liquid dish soap, cover the bottom of pan with water, and bring to a boil. Or lightly cover the bottom of the pan with baking soda. Add water to a depth of ½ inch (12 millimeters) and ½ cup vinegar. Bring to a boil, turn off the heat, and leave overnight. Rinse well.

· · · · ·

To renew stainless steel pots and pans, put them into a heavy duty black plastic bag. Pour 1–2 cups of ammonia into the bag. Close the bag tightly and place it in a sunny, outside location for 4–8 hours. Averting your face, open the bag quickly and fully and leave for a few minutes. Use a garden hose to rinse off and dilute the ammonia. Wash the pans immediately with hot soapy water. Do not use this method on anodized aluminum, aluminum, or cast iron pans. It can be used to clean grill grates and oven racks.

· · · ·

To remove stains from stainless steel pans, apply ketchup to the pan and scrub with a nylon scouring pad. Ketchup on a non-abrasive pad can also be used on brass and chrome.

· · · ·

Citric acid, bleach, and vinegar should not be left on stainless steel for an extended period of time because they may leave permanent marks.

· · · ·

If a frying pan has become discolored, boil apple peel in it for a few minutes, then rinse and dry.

· · · ·

A greasy cast-iron pan will wash easily; first shake salt over the pan and wipe out with a paper towel. Wash in warm water using a nylon scouring pad. Season by coating with cooking oil and heating in the oven at a low temperature for an hour.

· · · ·

Soak a rusted cast iron pan overnight in a solution of 2 parts white vinegar to 1 part water to remove the rust. Rub stubborn stains with a ball of aluminum foil dipped in salt. Wipe clean with a soft cloth.

· · · ·

To clean the black marks off pots and pans or range hood filters, mix enough white vinegar with cream of tartar to make a paste. Scrub with a nonabrasive pad. Tough marks may need the paste left on for a few minutes.

· · · ·

Remove a buildup of grease on enamel pans by covering the bottom of the pan with a layer of powdered detergent, then cover with a wet towel and leave for a few hours. Rinse off thoroughly.

· · · ·

To remove burned food from enamel cookware cover the bottom of the pan with a solution of water and 4–5 tablespoons of salt. Leave to soak overnight then bring to a boil and the debris will come away easily.

· · · ·

Give metal or aluminum pans a shine by rubbing them with a paste of one part salt and one part vinegar, then warm up over low heat.

· · · ·

Clean aluminum pots and pans with ammonia-free detergent and water.

· · · ·

To brighten up an aluminum pot, boil 2 pints (1 liter) water in it with 4 tablespoons white vinegar, cream of tartar, apple peel, or onion for a few minutes, then rinse and dry well.

. . . .

Place a dryer sheet and warm water in crusted pots and pans overnight. Then use the dryer sheet to wipe clean.

. . . .

Saw off the rounded end of a wooden spoon to make a good strong scraper that will not damage the surface of pans.

. . . .

Invest in a three-tiered steamer pan; a whole meal can be cooked using one ring of the cooker.

. . . .

To remove tough stains from ceramic or enamel cookware, soak for 1–2 hours in hot water, baking soda, and detergent. This will make the stain easier to remove.

. . . .

Put a spoon or jar lid in the bottom pan of a double boiler; the rattle will give an alarm that the water is running low.

. . . .

When cooking over a wood fire, cover the base of the pan with a film of soap for easier cleaning.

. . . .

To remove the dark rings inside a saucepan left after boiling eggs, boil water and a slice of lemon in the pan.

. . . .

Easily line baking pans with aluminum foil by turning the pan upside down and pressing a sheet of heavy-duty aluminum foil around it, then remove foil, turn the pan over, and drop foil inside. Crimp edges of foil to rim of pan.

. . . .

Pour 1 tablespoon water into the unfilled spaces of a cupcake tin to help preserve the life of the pan.

. . . .

Hard-to-remove rust stains on baking tins can be scoured with half a raw potato and powdered detergent.

SMALL UTENSILS

Before using a can opener, dip it in very hot water and it will cut more easily and evenly.

. . . .

To clean an electric can opener, remove the cutting wheel and lid holder and soak them in soapy water. If they cannot be removed, scrub with an old, clean toothbrush and a powdered cleanser. Rinse thoroughly.

. . . .

Wash can openers with full strength vinegar or ammonia to cut down on buildup of debris. Use an old toothbrush dipped in vinegar to clean around the blade.

. . . .

A vacuum flask can be cleaned by adding 3 tablespoons baking soda and warm water, then shaking gently. Leave to stand for 15 minutes, rinse well, and leave to dry.

. . . .

Keep a spray bottle with a solution of 1 part bleach to 4 parts water, or an all-purpose spray cleaner in the kitchen for wiping down after meals.

. . . .

Spray a colander with nonstick vegetable spray before using to drain pasta, or rinse with cold water after use.

. . . .

Clean a garlic press after each use with a toothbrush and rinse with hot water to prevent the garlic from drying on it.

"The shortest way to do many things is to do only one thing at a time."
—Richard Cech

Clean cheese graters with a vegetable brush. For easier cleaning coat the grater with salad oil before use.

. . . .

When using a chopping board, place a damp tea towel underneath to prevent it from slipping on the work surface.

. . . .

To clean a wooden cutting board, cover it with bleach and salt and scrub with a stiff brush. Rinse well with very hot water and dry with a clean cloth. Season the board with a mineral oil. Do not use vegetable oil as it can turn rancid.

. . . .

Or pour vinegar onto the wood and, wiping in the direction of the wood grain, use a sponge to remove the grime.

. . . .

To brighten chopping boards, after washing them with soap and water, rub the boards with a damp cloth dipped in salt.

. . . .

Before applying mineral oil (e.g., paraffin oil) to a butcher's block, warm the oil slightly and apply with a soft cloth, rubbing in the direction of the grain. Allow the oil to soak in between each of the 4–5 coats required for the initial seasoning. After each treatment, wait 4–6 hours and wipe off any excess oil. Re-oil the butcher block monthly or as often as needed.

. . . .

Clean cork coasters and mats by washing them in cold water and scrubbing with a pumice stone. Rinse with cold water and put them in a cool, dry place until they are dry.

. . . .

To revive scratched and dull dark wooden dishes, make a thick paste of instant coffee and water and rub the stain with a clean sponge or cloth; wipe off any excess.

. . . .

Restore the original glow to a wooden salad bowl and wooden utensils by rubbing them with vegetable oil. Leave overnight, then wipe off the excess oil.

. . . .

Rubbing waxed paper over the inside and outside of a wooden salad bowl will prevent it from becoming sticky.

. . . .

To prevent new wooden utensils from absorbing food odors, soak them overnight in white vinegar before using.

. . . .

If it is difficult to read the raised markings on a measuring spoon, paint red nail polish over the measurements. Sand lightly and the numbers will stand out clearly.

. . . .

After washing salt and pepper shakers, dry them with a hair dryer to prevent the seasonings from clumping when the shakers are refilled. Never store shakers or spices near heat.

. . . .

"Half our life is spent trying to find something to do with the time we have rushed through life trying to save." —Unknown

After decorating a cake, boil all cake decorating tips and spatulas in vinegar and water to remove the grease.

. . . .

Stick the ends of skewers stored in a kitchen drawer into two corks so there are no accidents while rummaging.

. . . .

When using metal skewers, use square or twisted types, which will hold the food better than round ones.

. . . .

Use a large flowerpot to store kitchen utensils. It can be painted or stencilled to suit the kitchen décor.

. . . .

Place the head of a squeeze sponge mop in a plastic bag to prevent it from drying out and cracking.

. . . .

Lemon juice added to boiling water when cleaning baby bottles will release clinging mineral deposits.

. . . .

When cooking with tongs, avoid making a mess by using a coffee or beer mug as a rest for the tongs.

. . . .

A good knife should be sturdy and well balanced. The end of the blade should extend to the end of the handle, where it is anchored by several rivets. It should be made of high-carbon stainless steel or forged carbon.

· · · ·

Never keep sharp knives in a drawer—their edges and tips get scratched and become dull.

· · · ·

If sharp knives must be stored in a drawer, make a sheath for each one using the flattened cardboard tube from foil or waxed paper rolls or use purchased knife sheaths.

· · · ·

A wooden chopping board is easier on a knife edge than a hard plastic board.

· · · ·

Depending on use, a knife requires sharpening only once or twice a year. Steel it frequently to maintain its sharp edge.

· · · ·

Sharpen a dull utility knife blade by running it across a smooth concrete block or on the unglazed base of a pottery mug. Hold the blade at a slight angle and slide it in one direction.

Stainless steel knives are too hard to be sharpened, while serrated knives require professional equipment.

. . . .

Sharp knives are safer to use than dull blades, which can easily slip from food and require more pressure to cut.

. . . .

Exposing a knife to high heat can permanently damage it.

. . . .

Some foods like onions, potatoes, and artichokes will discolor carbon knives; conversely, the knives will also discolor the food.

. . . .

Stainless steel knives will stay shiny if they are rubbed with a slice of lemon peel or with alcohol on a dampened rag. Wash before using.

. . . .

When shopping for a knife rack, choose one made of wood, either a free-standing or a wall model. Wood is much kinder to knives than the magnetic holders because it does not abrade the blade.

Plastic & Glass Ware

To remove a residual odor of onions or garlic from a plastic storage container, wash and pack with pieces of newspaper, seal, and leave overnight or longer if required. Or soak a sponge in a mixture of equal parts vinegar and water. Place the sponge in the container overnight.

. . . .

Keep plastic ware odor free and disinfected by soaking it in a solution of baking soda and hot water.

. . . .

To eliminate staining, spray plastic containers with a nonstick cooking spray before pouring in a tomato-based sauce.

. . . .

To clean plastic that has been used to store sauce, wash in cold water and detergent first. Then rinse and wash as usual. Hot water only causes the plastic to retain the stain.

. . . .

Stained plastic dishes and pottery should be soaked for a few minutes in a solution of ¾ cup chlorine bleach, ¼ cup baking soda, and 1 cup vinegar. Wash as usual.

. . . .

Rub scratched or well-worn plastic plates and glasses with toothpaste and rinse in warm water.

. . . .

If closing the seals on a plastic box is difficult, run it under hot water for 20 seconds and then snap closed.

. . . .

Rigid plastic lids from small containers make good separators for frozen hamburger patties.

. . . .

Empty plastic liners from cereal boxes make good freezer bags or wax paper or use as lunch bags. Use when breading meats and vegetables or when pounding meat.

. . . . .

Seal any plastic bag by placing a piece of aluminum foil over the end to be sealed and running a hot iron over the foil. The foil must be equal on both sides of the plastic to be sealed so it does not stick to the ironing surface.

. . . . .

Cut out a hole in the side of a plastic milk jug and use to store plastic grocery bags.

. . . . .

Protect outdoor plastic furniture with a coat of car wax.

. . . . .

To prevent bags of flour from splitting when stored in a cupboard, cut a clean plastic milk container in half and put the base of the flour bag into it.

. . . . .

To remove wrinkles from a plastic table cover, place it in the dryer with a wet towel on high heat for a couple of minutes to soften and make it pliable. Place cover over the table and pull out the wrinkles. Watch carefully so it does not melt.

. . . . .

Before using new glasses, soak them in warm salty water for a few hours to help prevent them from cracking.

. . . .

To separate two stuck drinking glasses, set the bottom glass in warm water and fill the top one with cold water.

. . . .

Keep a drinking glass from cracking as it is filled with hot liquid by resting a metal spoon in it.

. . . .

To sterilize beer glasses, fill them with warm water and heat in microwave until boiling, remove when cool, drain, and allow to self-dry. Never put milk into beer glasses as it leaves a film.

. . . .

Glassware that has held milk should be rinsed in cold water before being immersed into hot soapy water.

For cloudy drinking glasses, soak them for 1 hour in slightly warm white vinegar. Use a plastic scrubber to remove film. If the glasses are still cloudy then they may have etching damage, which is permanent.

. . . .

Make inexpensive glassware sparkle by cleaning with a thin paste of baking soda and water and rubbing it onto the glass. Rinse well in cold running water, dry, and polish with a soft cloth. Or sprinkle a little salt into the water.

. . . .

WD-40 will take off almost any residue from stickers on glass and other surfaces. Or dab them with cooking oil and leave overnight before scrubbing.

. . . .

Use salt and lemon juice to clean glass containers. If the glass is not fragile, swirl crushed ice around until container is clean, then rinse with warm water.

. . . .

Clean glassware with stale tea. If they spot, soak in buttermilk, let dry, and wipe off.

. . . .

To remove a film from glasses or lamp globes add 2 tablespoons household ammonia to the dishwater.

. . . .

Put crumpled kitchen paper inside washed and dried twist-top jam jars when storing them to absorb any moisture and stop the lid corroding.

. . . .

Use latex gloves to give a nonslip grip when opening jars. Or wrap a rubber band around the lid to improve the grip.

. . . .

If a lid is hard to open, wrap a cloth soaked in hot water around it or set the jar upside down in a saucer and pour in enough hot water to cover the lid. Leave for a few minutes, dry off, and it should open easily. Or, first bang the flat top of the jar firmly on a hard surface.

Fixtures & Fittings

Formica worktops can be cleaned with mild liquid scouring cleaner, baking soda, or a glass cleaner. Wipe with a damp sponge, rinse, and wipe dry. For stubborn spots, apply laundry prewash spray or a paste of baking soda and water. Leave for 30 minutes, then rub with a plastic scrubber. For a greasy stain, use a little rubbing alcohol.

. . . .

Use car polish to clean scratched kitchen worktops and counters, allow to dry a little and then buff off.

. . . .

For coffee rings or spilled drink stains on countertops, rub a little dishwasher liquid on the spot with fingertips. Leave for a few minutes and wipe thoroughly with a damp cloth.

. . . .

In a small kitchen with limited counter space pull out two top drawers and cover them with a cutting board or baking sheet to give extra workspace.

. . . . .

To remove scratches or watermarks from antique or modern wood furniture and leave a soft sheen combine 1 teaspoon instant coffee and 2 teaspoons water. Go over the surface with the mixture using a small wad of cotton. Polish as usual.

. . . . .

Use kerosene to remove black stains from fire tools or ash marks on a cold fireplace. Wash off with soap and water.

. . . . .

Clean up grease or oil spills easily by sprinkling flour over the spill to prevent it spreading when wiping it up.

. . . . .

Clean painted cabinets by mixing together 1 cup white vinegar, 2 cups ammonia, ½ cup baking soda, and 2 gallons (10 liters) warm water. Use rubber gloves.

. . . . .

Spray a little window cleaner on a soft, lint-free cloth and use it to clean the TV screen. Never spray a cleanser directly onto the screen.

. . . . .

To flatten a curling rug, place a damp towel underneath the rug, put a heavy weight on top, and leave overnight.

. . . . .

To remove pet hair add a little liquid fabric softener to water, spray lightly on fabric, leave to dry, then vacuum or brush off. Or add the fabric softener to cleaning solution when mopping the floor or wiping counters. Any hair will mop up easily.

. . . . .

Soap can discolor cane, rush, bamboo, and matting. Clean these with a strong saltwater solution instead. Greasy marks can be removed by adding a little ammonia to the water. Remaining marks can be treated with methylated spirits.

. . . . .

To clean greasy furniture, use a solution of 1 tablespoon borax and warm water.

. . . . .

Leather furniture should be cleaned with two parts linseed oil and one part vinegar. To brighten leather use the white of an egg and rub with a soft dry cloth.

. . . . .

Oak furniture can be cleaned with warm beer.

. . . . .

To clean and polish wood surfaces, blend together ¼ pint (125 milliliters) strained lemon juice, ½ pint (250 milliliters) raw linseed oil, and 10 drops of pure lemon oil. Store in a pump spray bottle and apply with a slightly moistened soft cloth.

. . . .

Apply spray starch to doors and painted walls in hallways and stairways. The coating will resist marks.

. . . .

Put cornstarch over greasy spills on a carpet, leave for 1 hour, then brush off.

. . . .

In freezing temperatures, add dishwashing liquid to warm water and pour over icy doorsteps to stop refreezing.

. . . .

To clean washable wallpaper, combine 1 cup warm water and ¼ cup liquid dishwashing detergent and beat to a stiff foam. Apply to the wallpaper with a sponge or cloth.

To remove the stains on wallpaper, rub with baking soda. For difficult stains use a solution of equal amounts of rubbing alcohol and water or use 2 tablespoons hydrogen peroxide per 1 gallon (5 liters) water. Wet the surface with the solution, then rinse thoroughly.

. . . .

For high gloss panelling, add 1 cup liquid floor wax to 1 gallon (5 liters) water. Wash with a soft cloth.

. . . .

To polish black cast iron, black painted steel, or chrome or nickel trim, especially on wood stoves, crumple a sheet of newspaper and dry scrub.

. . . .

Put a layer of old newspaper, brown paper, or wallpaper on top of kitchen units. It saves having to clean off stubborn grease. Throw away and replace the paper as required.

. . . .

For a quick facelift to a kitchen, change the handles on drawers and cabinets. Paste motifs randomly on plain tiles.

. . . .

To remove a smoke film from walls, make a solution of ½ cup borax, 2 tablespoons soap flakes, 1 tablespoon ammonia, and 1 gallon (5 liters) warm water. Use full strength in a spray bottle or add 2 cups to a bucket of warm water.

. . . .

Clean the fireplace bricks by using warm soapy water mixed with 8 ounces (200 grams) powdered pumice and ½ cup household ammonia. Scrub well with a scrubbing brush. Rinse thoroughly by sponging with plenty of water. Clean dirty grouting with a smoker's toothpaste or whitewall cleaner. Keep bricks clean by sealing them with a sealant or paint using a heat-resistant paint.

. . . .

To quick-shine floors after they have been swept clean, use a mop with a piece of wax paper underneath. The remaining dust will stick to the paper.

. . . .

Sweep or vacuum a floor thoroughly before mopping. Mop in a figure eight pattern to make the chore less tiring. Run a portable fan at one end of the room to dry a floor quickly.

. . . .

To clean yellow waxy buildup off a vinyl floor, wash the area with cool, clear water only. Scrub with warm water only on the areas that get the most wear and tear.

. . . .

For scuff marks or stains on vinyl tile, dab a cloth in turpentine, rub the mark away, then rinse. Another option is to rub the mark with a pencil eraser.

. . . .

To shine a kitchen floor, add sour milk to the rinse water.

. . . .

For laminated floors, add ¼ cup vinegar to a liter spray bottle and fill with water. Spray a small area of the floor with the solution and wipe with a damp terry mop.

. . . . .

Use tea to clean wood furniture and hardwood floors. Brew two teabags in four cups of water and allow it to cool to lukewarm. Soak a cloth in the tea, then squeeze until damp and use to clean the wood. The tannic acid in the tea cleans the wood. It will also remove furniture polish buildup.

THIS & THAT

As food wrap is used, tearing it off becomes more difficult because there is less weight to the roll, so there is nothing to pull against. To fix this, put a piece of heavy pipe inside the roll to give the weight needed to make it easier to tear.

. . . . .

Put potpourri into the foot of a pair of tights, tie a knot, and place behind a radiator. The heat brings out the fragrance.

. . . . .

Make a dust cloth by soaking cloth in 2 pints (1.2 liters) water with 2 teaspoons turpentine added and allow to dry.

. . . . .

For homemade scouring powder combine 1 cup borax, 1 cup baking soda, and 1 cup salt.

. . . .

Pet hair clings to broom bristles sprayed with furniture polish.

. . . .

Soy sauce bottles with the shaker lid make great containers for vinegar or strong sauces.

. . . .

Always keep a bunch of clothes pegs in the cupboard; they are very useful to secure bags closed.

. . . .

Store steel-wool pads in clay pots, or add baking soda to their storage dish, or place the used pad on a piece of aluminum foil. Prevent steel-wool pads from getting rusty by storing them in a plastic zip bag in the freezer. Remove from the freezer and run under tap water when required.

. . . .

Coat the wall behind the stove with furniture polish. It will make it easier to wipe clean.

. . . .

Attach an old sock to a fly swatter with a rubber band and use to dust under hard-to-reach places and under furniture.

. . . .

To keep drains unblocked, pour coffee dregs down them.

. . . .

For drain cleaner, add 1 cup baking soda to 1 cup hot vinegar and pour down the drain. Wait a few minutes, then flush the drain with 2 pints (1.2 liters) of very hot water.

. . . .

To help just-dry-cleaned curtains stay fresh and crisp, spray them with a few coats of unscented hair spray before hanging. Allow drapes to dry between applications.

. . . .

Sprinkle borax on carpets to get rid of fleas, leave for a few days, and then vacuum it up. Or scatter eucalyptus leaves around the room—fleas do not like the smell of them.

. . . .

Clean an aquarium with non-iodized salt and a heavy-duty plastic pot scrubber. Rinse well.

. . . .

To clean an interior waterfall or water sculpture, disconnect and drain. Scrub with baking soda and if there is resistant mildew, wash with vinegar.

. . . .

Wrap a flashlight in fluorescent tape so that it is easily located when there is a power outage.

. . . .

To prevent torch batteries from corroding, place aluminum foil between the spring and the end cap.

. . . .

To remove a cork from inside an empty wine bottle, pour some ammonia into the bottle and set it in a well-ventilated location. In a few days the cork will be disintegrated.

. . . .

Remove wine stains from a decanter by mixing some chopped raw potato with warm water, then add to the decanter and shake vigorously. Rinse well.

. . . .

To dry a washed wine decanter thoroughly, aim a hairdryer inside; do not let it come in contact with wet surfaces.

. . . .

If red wine is spilled on a carpet, it may be cleaned with shaving cream or soda water, then sponge off with water.

. . . .

Sprinkle some kitty litter in the bottom of the kitchen garbage can to help absorb odors and catch drips.

. . . .

Spray garbage bags with ammonia to discourage dogs from tearing bags before pickup.

Before cleaning or buying a piece of brass it is useful to find out whether it is solid brass or if it is plated. To do this, place a magnet against the surface; if it is plated the magnet will stick, if it is solid brass it will not stick. Over-cleaning plated brass can remove some of the finish.

· · · · ·

Clean brass with hot soapy water and a soft cloth. An old toothbrush will help out in tight spots. If the piece is slightly tarnished use a jeweller's cloth or wadding polish.

· · · · ·

To clean copper, pour sour milk into a flat dish and soak the copper in it for an hour, clean as usual. Or rub copper with a lemon and salt mixture and dry with a soft cloth.

· · · · ·

To bleach green algae stains from coral, shells, or any aquarium decoration, soak in a mild bleach solution until white. Rinse well under running water. Soak for 24 hours in a plastic container filled with water and a small bottle of aquarium water chlorine remover.

· · · · ·

Old lined rubber gloves make excellent silver cleaners. Simply turn them inside out and use the lining to polish silver. Use the inside skin of a banana to polish silverware.

· · · · ·

Polish chrome with methylated spirits, remove rust with aluminum foil. To shine, rub with baking soda.

· · · · ·

To remove rust stains from sinks and tubs, pour a few drops of hydrogen peroxide on the stain and sprinkle it with cream of tartar. Leave for 30 minutes, then wipe off with a sponge.

. . . . .

Make a paste with mustard and spread on the back of a loose tile to secure it to the wall.

. . . . .

Attach a magnetic strip to the inside of a medicine cabinet door to hold tweezers, nail clippers, or small scissors.

. . . . .

A cloth wrung out in 1 tablespoon cornstarch dissolved in 2 pints (1.2 liters) water will make windows and mirrors sparkle.

. . . . .

Fill a spray bottle with equal amounts of vinegar and water for a great window and mirror cleaner.

. . . . .

Use vertical strokes when washing windows outside and horizontal for inside windows to show any streaks. Do not wash windows on a sunny day. They will dry too quickly.

. . . . .

To test for hard water, add ½ teaspoon detergent to 2 pints (1.2 liters) warm water in a jar, close it, and shake vigorously. If it does not foam up, or suds disappear quickly, the water is hard.

. . . . .

To soften hard water, combine 8 ounces (200 grams) washing soda and 4 ounces (100 grams) borax with 1 gallon (5 liters) water. Store in labelled plastic bottles. Add 1 cup of the solution to each wash.

. . . . .

To remove stains from tea towels, fill the washer with water, put in the usual amount of detergent, and add ½ cup automatic dishwashing detergent. This will remove most stains.

. . . . .

For dingy, gray dishcloths, soak them in 2 tablespoons cream of tartar or borax dissolved in hot water, then wash as usual.

. . . . .

To keep salt from clogging in the shaker, add ½ teaspoon uncooked rice.

. . . . .

To remember something for the next day, put a note in the shoes you will be wearing.

. . . . .

To clean artificial flowers, pour some salt into a paper bag and add the flowers. Shake vigorously and the salt will absorb all the dust, leaving the flowers looking like new.

STOCKING A KITCHEN

Create an herb rack or make cupboard space for spices and herbs. Get started with: salt and pepper, chili powder, basil, oregano, rosemary, thyme, bay leaves, cayenne pepper, red pepper flakes, cumin, curry powder, ginger, nutmeg, and cinnamon.

. . . . .

Keep baking supplies handy, such as flour, brown and white sugar, baking powder or baking soda, cornstarch, and vanilla extract. In addition to baking, these are used for creating and thickening sauces and sweetening beverages.

• • • •

Honey: for sweetening certain batters and other mixtures.

• • • •

Varieties of fruit jams or preserves are useful for glazing tarts or piecrusts.

• • • •

Nonstick vegetable spray is useful to prevent batters and other foods from sticking to a pan or baking sheet.

• • • •

Stock the refrigerator and cupboards with condiments such as stock cubes, mayonnaise, ketchup, mustards, jams, and other spreads. Black olives, pickles, capers, and spicy sauces can jazz up meals.

Keep nuts and seeds around. They are great in cookies and cakes, pastas, salads, and for snacking.

. . . .

Keep a selection of cheese including a grating cheese, like Parmesan— for instant tasty protein.

. . . .

Store dried pastas, rice, cereals, potatoes, and other durable grains. Their value is limitless.

. . . .

Always have garlic and onions available.

. . . .

Keep oils for frying and salad dressings. Store red wine, white wine, balsamic and malt vinegar for vinaigrettes and whenever a little acidity is needed.

. . . .

Have one bottle of dry white wine and one bottle of red wine, for both cooking and drinking.

. . . .

Buy canned and jars of staples for use when in a pinch. Tuna, canned beans, and sauces can start off any kitchen creation. Canned tomatoes are indispensable for quick pasta sauces.

. . . .

Keep portions of meat, poultry, and fish in the freezer as well as some frozen vegetables.

Cooking Conundrums

SHOPPING

Groceries are one of the few flexible items in a family budget, but it can sometimes be challenging to find creative ways to save on regular family food costs.

. . . .

Plan ahead whether cooking meals ahead of time to store in the freezer or just planning a menu and shopping lists in advance.

. . . .

Set a grocery budget and then make sure menus and grocery lists fit this budget.

. . . .

Plan meals around items already on hand and around offers in local grocery stores. Buy produce when it is in season.

. . . .

Shop with cash. This is a surprisingly effective means of staying on budget.

. . . .

Do not shop when hungry as it can result in impulse purchases— especially junk food.

. . . .

Keep a running total of how much is spent at the store. Do not go over the amount budgeted for.

. . . .

Keep a note of the cheapest prices of regularly purchased items.

. . . . .

A simple rule of thumb when shopping is "look high, look low." Shops often place expensive items at eye level.

. . . . .

Convenience food costs more than food prepared at home. Use convenience foods as little as possible.

. . . . .

Only use coupons for those items and brands normally purchased—it's not usually prudent to buy an item just because you have a coupon. Always check the expiration date on coupons.

. . . . .

Stock up on frequently used items when they are on sale. Only bulk buy perishable foods if there is space in the freezer to store any excess.

. . . . .

Watch for sales on ground meats. Divide the meat into 1 pound (450 grams) batches and freeze in individual zip-top freezer bags. Lower grades of meat and poultry are usually just as nutritious and cost less.

. . . . .

Check the label of perishable foods for last recommended date of use. Avoid buying items nearing this date to have more time to use them before they perish.

. . . . .

When shopping, especially in warm weather, always purchase perishables last and, if possible, pack in a cooler bag or box. Refrigerate as soon as possible.

COOKING

Read a couple of good cookbooks from cover to cover.

. . . .

Keep loose recipes in a 3-ring binder. Organize the recipes into categories and store the binder with the cookbooks. Jot down comments and modifications as you experiment.

. . . .

To keep a recipe book open use a pants clip hanger to clamp the book open at the page required and hang it up at eye level on a cupboard doorknob. A handy holder for a loose recipe can also be made by standing a fork turned upside down in a glass; the recipe fits into the fork prongs.

. . . .

Keep recipes clean and easy to use by storing them in small photo albums. They stay open and lie flat and the pages can be wiped off easily. They are especially good for recipes printed on thin paper from magazines or newspapers.

When using recipe cards, cut a slit across the top of a cork at a slight angle. Slip the recipe card into the slit. The recipe can be easily followed.

. . . .

To ensure success with any recipe, read the recipe from beginning to end. Make a note of any preparations that need to be made ahead of time. Save time by assembling ingredients and utensils before beginning.

. . . .

Make sure the oven is preheated to required temperature if the recipe calls for it.

. . . .

It is not always necessary to preheat the oven. If cooking time is less than an hour, then 5 minutes of preheating will do. If the cooking time is more than 1 hour, just turn on the oven when the dish is placed inside.

. . . .

Clean as you go in the kitchen. Keep a clean, wet soapy rag to wipe the work area regularly.

. . . .

Before working with messy foods, cover the countertop or sink with waxed paper or newspaper to catch the mess. When finished, wad up the paper and discard.

. . . .

Never buy or use food in leaking, bulging or dented cans, cracked jars, or jars with loose or bulging lids.

. . . .

Once opened, cans should not be used to store food. Lead may leach from the cans into the contents, especially if the food contains acid.

. . . .

Preparation is usually more time consuming in stir frying than in sautéing or pan-frying. In stir frying, high heat is used to cook meat and vegetables quickly in a small amount of oil.

. . . .

A meal can be cooked on one burner using a steamer. Start off with meat in the bottom with stock. Twenty minutes prior to dishing up the meal put vegetables in the top and steam to perfection.

. . . .

If using the oven for roasting meat, utilize the rest of the oven. Cook roast potatoes and make a dessert like a rice pudding.

. . . .

To cool an oven, put a large heatproof basin of cold water in and it will instantly cool.

. . . .

Turn off the oven several minutes before a dish is done and let the remaining heat finish the cooking.

. . . .

"Cooking is like love.
It should be entered into with abandon or not at all."—Unknown

When cooking a dish, double the quantity and freeze half.

· · · ·

When cooking over a gas stove, adjust the flame so that it just touches the bottom of the pot and does not go over the sides. The flame should be blue and cone shaped.

· · · ·

When using an electric stove, use a pot that is about the same size or a little bigger than the element.

· · · ·

To keep cooked food warm but not overcook it, remove from the heat and make a tent of foil, shiny side down, over the food.

· · · ·

Always set the timer 5–10 minutes earlier than what the recipe calls for. Oven temperatures vary, so leaving a dish in for too long can cause overcooking.

· · · ·

When the specific casserole baking dish called for in a recipe is not available, use a pan of equal or slightly greater volume. Use water to measure the volume of casserole dishes.

· · · ·

Casseroles really taste best when made in advance. Time will allow the flavors to blossom.

· · · ·

Use a lid on a pot to reduce cooking time. A dish can still simmer in the heat that remains immediately after it is turned off.

. . . .

When lifting the lid of a cooking pot, open it outward to prevent a blast of steam from hitting your face.

. . . .

Place a wooden spoon across the top of the pot when boiling water. It separates the steam and keeps it from boiling over.

. . . .

To hasten the cooking of foods in a double boiler, add salt to the water in the outer boiler.

. . . .

Never fill a pressure cooker with more food than half its capacity if the contents are mainly liquid, or two-thirds if the contents are mainly solid.

. . . .

To avoid burns, use thick, dry potholders as wet potholders will allow the heat to soak through.

. . . .

Spray the spatula with nonstick spray to prevent foods sticking to it.

If a dish has turned out too sweet, squeeze a lemon or lime into it. If the dish contains milk or milk products, simply add salt. Alcohol will also soak up unwanted sweetness.

. . . .

For an easy dip for potato chips or raw vegetables, beat a little salad dressing and tomato ketchup into cream cheese. Quantities depend on taste, color, and texture required.

. . . .

Make filling taco shells easy by using a muffin tin. Turn the tin upside down and fit the shells in the spaces. The shells will stand upright, making it easy to fill them.

. . . .

If serving buffet style, position everything so guests can help themselves from both sides of the table. Place napkins and eating utensils at the end of the line rather than the beginning. This gives everyone that extra hand to serve him or herself.

. . . .

If guests are coming but dinner is late, throw some onions on to sauté and the kitchen will smell of tasty food.

. . . .

To baste food, fill a squeeze bottle with barbecue sauce or marinade and squeeze directly onto foods while grilling, reducing cleanup.

. . . .

For an outdoor party or barbecue, line a wheelbarrow with a sheet of plastic, fill it with ice, and pack the drinks into it. Wheel it to a shady location close by and it saves running back and forth to fetch drinks.

. . . . .

Grocery bags make great refrigerator storage containers for large bowls of food. Put the bowl or pan at the bottom of the bag and pull the bag up over the sides and tie it.

. . . . .

To measure small liquid amounts, use a medicine measure.

. . . . .

For creamy oatmeal, soak the oats in cold milk overnight. Coat the cooking pan with nonstick cooking spray to keep the oatmeal from boiling over and sticking to the pan.

. . . . .

Salt added to water makes the water boil at a higher temperature, thus reducing cooking time. It does not make the water boil faster.

. . . . .

For a salt substitute, combine 3 teaspoons each dry mustard, garlic, and onion powder, 3 teaspoons paprika, 1½ teaspoons pepper or cayenne, 1 teaspoon basil, and 1 teaspoon thyme. Store in a covered shaker bottle.

. . . . .

All dried spices should be crushed before using. This brings out their aromatic flavor and helps it absorb into the food.

. . . . .

To help bring out the flavor of spices before adding them to a favorite recipe, toast them for 30 seconds in a dry pan over medium heat until they release their aromas, or they can be sautéed in a small amount of oil for 20–30 seconds.

. . . . .

Before using kitchen scissors to halve marshmallows or dates, coat with nonstick vegetable spray.

. . . . .

Rub grater with oil before using it and it will easily wipe clean.

. . . . .

Always spray the grill with nonstick cooking spray before grilling to avoid sticking.

. . . . .

To quickly use that frozen juice concentrate, mash it with a potato masher.

. . . . .

The inside waxed paper bags from cereal boxes are useful, especially for keeping lettuce crisp.

. . . . .

For neat and tidy grating, hold the hand grater and whatever is being grated inside a large plastic bag while grating.

. . . . .

To prevent drips when pouring from a jug, place a dab of butter or margarine under the spout.

. . . . .

When handling hot ramekins, wrap the ends of tongs with rubber bands and they will not slip around.

. . . .

Rub vinegar over hands before cooking to prevent odors from staining them.

. . . .

To remove odors from hands, rub them with a stainless steel object, such as a spoon, under running water.

. . . .

To prevent mold forming on top of tomato paste, wipe down the inside of the can with a paper towel to the unused portion. Pour a thin film of oil over the surface of the paste to stop air reaching the surface. Store paste in the refrigerator and simply spoon out as much as you need.

. . . .

Alternatively, freeze paste in level-tablespoon portions in ice cube trays. When the paste is frozen, transfer to a bag and seal tightly.

. . . .

To easily get ketchup out of a bottle, insert a drinking straw, push it to the bottom of the bottle, and then remove. Enough air will be admitted to start an even flow. Do not hit the bottom of a sauce bottle or shake it vertically. Shake it from side to side until you can see that the contents have started flowing.

. . . .

To strain fat off quickly, pour it through a coffee filter.

. . . .

When covering a bowl or pan with plastic wrap, moisten the rim and it will adhere better.

. . . . .

To toast sesame seeds, sprinkle a thin layer of sesame seeds in a pan and shake or stir over low heat until they are a golden color.

. . . . .

Turmeric can be substituted for the more expensive saffron in recipes. The taste will be slightly different, but the color will be just as golden.

. . . . .

Sugar and acidic foods, such as tomatoes, tend to have a hardening effect on beans; therefore, always soften beans thoroughly before using them in baked beans, chili, and similar recipes.

. . . . .

Place tins of baked beans or soup upside down when storing to avoid the liquid settling at the top.

If it is difficult to turn the key on a can of sardines, push the handle of a teaspoon through the key, twist the spoon around, and the lid will come off easily.

. . . .

Use a piece of bread as a spoon rest. The heel works best.

. . . .

To keep salad dressing from going rancid, put a little sugar into it.

. . . .

To chill foods quickly, put them in the freezer for 20–30 minutes rather than longer in the refrigerator.

. . . .

Make Thousand Island Dressing by adding a little tomato purée to mayonnaise.

. . . .

When pickling beets, boil the vinegar, leave to cool, and add 2 tablespoons sweet sherry to the liquid.

. . . .

Before making oatmeal, lightly rub the inside of the saucepan with butter. It will be easier to clean afterwards.

. . . .

Stir 1–2 teaspoons mint jelly into iced tea for a refreshing twist.

. . . .

*"Cookery is not chemistry. It is an art.
It requires instinct and taste rather than exact measurements."*
—Marcel Boulestin

Place a sugar lump into a cookie jar to keep the cookies crisp.

. . . . .

Honey is best stored in a dry place because it tends to absorb moisture and become granulated. Or it can be kept in small containers in the freezer to prevent sugaring.

. . . . .

To easily remove honey from a measuring spoon, first coat the spoon with nonstick cooking spray. Honey also removes easily when you run hot water on the spoon.

. . . . .

Old or badly stored popcorn kernels may lose their ability to pop. Popping requires the presence of adequate moisture. To revive dried-out popcorn kernels, add 1 tablespoon water to a 2-pint (1.2-liter) jar of kernels and shake. Store in the refrigerator and leave until all the water is absorbed before popping.

. . . . .

Keep popcorn fresh and encourage more kernels to pop by storing it in the freezer.

. . . . .

Popcorn pops better when sprinkled with warm water an hour before use.

. . . . .

Add a cup of water to the bottom portion of the grilling pan before sliding into the oven to absorb smoke and grease.

. . . .

Tofu or bean curd is solidified soymilk. If tofu must be kept longer than a week, replace the liquid in the container with fresh water every day. Several minutes of parboiling or deep-frying revives tired tofu.

. . . .

Make peanut butter by adding a bag of salted, shelled peanuts into a food processor and blending with 1 tablespoon vegetable oil. Stop at the crunchy stage if preferred or keep the blade spinning till the mixture's smooth.

PASTA & RICE

When purchasing pasta, fresh or dried, be sure it is made with semolina or durum wheat. It absorbs less water and also has better flavor.

. . . .

Dried pasta will keep for up to 1 year when stored in an airtight container in a cool dry place.

. . . .

When preparing pasta as a main dish, plan for 2 ounces (50 grams) pasta per person; hearty eaters may require 4 ounces (100 grams).

. . . .

Place a wooden spoon across the pot when cooking pasta and it will not boil over.

．．．．

Cook pasta in salted water, but do not add the salt until the water boils. Use 2 tablespoons coarse salt to each 1 pound (450 grams) pasta. Once pasta is in the boiling water, stir and cover until water starts to boil again. Remove cover and cook until al dente, or firm to the bite, yet cooked through. Stir occasionally.

．．．．

When pasta is cooked "al dente" the flavor remains and is not cooked out and it is easier to digest.

．．．．

Stir pasta well when it is first put into the boiling water so it will not stick to itself or to the pan.

．．．．

For perfect pasta and hardboiled eggs, get water to a rolling boil, turn off heat, and leave for 15 minutes.

．．．．

Put a few drops of vinegar in pasta as it boils to make the pasta less sticky.

．．．．

Drain pasta as soon as it is cooked but never over-drain. If cooked pasta sticks together, spray it gently with hot running water for just a few seconds. Drain.

．．．．

"The ambition of every good cook must be to make something very good with the fewest possible ingredients." —Urbain Dubois

Do not rinse pasta unless specified. Rinsing cools the pasta too quickly and removes the surface starch that helps the sauce adhere.

· · · · ·

When the pasta comes out soft and bloated, the most likely reason is that it has been in the water too long. This happens if it is put into water that is not yet boiling, or alternatively if you keep the heat too low and the water does not boil during the cooking.

· · · · ·

Toss pasta with a dry grated cheese, such as Parmesan, before adding the sauce. The grated cheese will stick to the pasta and allow the sauce to cling to the pasta better.

· · · · ·

Pasta should be rinsed after draining only when it is being used in a cold dish, or when it is not going to be sauced and served immediately. In those cases, rinse the pasta under cold water to stop the cooking process and drain well.

· · · · ·

Spaghetti or tagliatelle tend to stick together when strained. Do not leave the pasta when you have strained it. Add either butter, oil, or the sauce immediately and stir it in well. If the sauce is fairly dry then add a ladle of the cooking water too.

· · · · ·

To quickly chill cooked pasta for salad, first drain the cooked pasta in a colander. Place the colander into a bigger bowl filled halfway with ice water. When chilled, lift the colander out of the ice water and drain.

. . . . .

To freeze cooked pasta, cool it slightly, then toss with a little olive oil or cooking oil. Spoon into airtight containers or freezer bags. Freeze for up to 2 weeks. Defrost a bag in a colander in the sink by running tepid water over it. Or drop the contents of the bag into boiling water. Thawing and warming time depends on the amount of pasta.

. . . . .

Do not break spaghetti in half before cooking. Broken spaghetti is too short to twirl on pasta utensils.

. . . . .

When cooking spaghetti or vermicelli, it is difficult to fish out a single strand to test for doneness. Using a serrated knife works well by catching the pasta on the serration.

. . . . .

Wait until the spaghetti stops steaming before serving to stop the steam condensing and wetting the plate.

Noodles, spaghetti, and other starches will not boil over if the inside of the pot is rubbed with vegetable oil.

. . . .

Two drops of yellow food coloring added to boiling noodles will make them look homemade.

. . . .

To keep noodles or rice from boiling over, add 1 tablespoon butter or oil to the water.

. . . .

Couscous is made from semolina that is rolled into small granules or pellets with a small quantity of salted water and sometimes flour. To cook, pour 1 cup couscous into 1 cup of boiling water. Remove from heat, cover, and let stand for 5 minutes. Fluff with a fork.

. . . .

Regular rice is available in long, medium, or short grains. Long grain rice cooks tender, with grains light, fluffy, and separated. It is usually used with savory dishes.

. . . .

Short and medium grain rice cooks plump and moist so that the grains tend to cling together. They are used in desserts and rice rings.

. . . .

Wild rice is referred to as rice. It is actually the seed of a water grass. It is cooked and served like rice.

. . . .

Each 1 cup of uncooked long-grain rice will make 3 cups of cooked rice.

. . . .

Use rice in almost any dish that calls for pasta.

. . . .

Always thoroughly wash and rinse any uncooked rice and repeat until the water runs clear before cooking with it. This removes the excess starch that causes it to stick together.

. . . .

Avoid stirring the rice as it cooks as this damages the grains and produces more starch in the water. A little oil, butter, or margarine in the water also helps reduce sticking.

. . . .

For fluffier, whiter rice, add 1 teaspoon lemon juice per 2 pints (1.2 liters) water. To add extra flavor and nutrition to rice, cook it in liquid reserved from cooking vegetables.

. . . .

Rice cooks better in low wide pots than high narrow ones.

. . . .

To cook rice in the microwave, place 2 cups rice and 4 cups of boiling water in a microwave dish and cook on high for 12 minutes. For 1 cup of rice use 2 cups of boiling water and microwave for 8 minutes.

. . . .

For better flavor and texture, cook rice in the amount of water
that will be absorbed during cooking.

· · · ·

To obtain the right amount of water to cook rice without
measuring, place a quantity of rice in a pot, shake the pot to
smooth out and settle the rice. Place the index finger lightly
on top of the rice, do not make a dent, add water until the first
knuckle is covered, about 1 inch (2.5 centimeters) above the
surface of the rice.

· · · ·

Keep cooked rice hot and fluffy by placing a slice of dry bread or
crumpled paper towel on top and cover with a lid.

· · · ·

To cook rice for stir frying, cook normally, then rinse with cold
water to cool quickly and safely. Rice should be completely cold
before stir-frying. Rice should be stir-fried over a high heat.
Reheated rice should always be served piping hot to eliminate
any risk from bacterial growth.

· · · ·

Make a crust for quiche with rice. Combine 1½ cups cooked rice
and ¼ cup shredded cheese and 1 egg. Pat lightly into a pie plate.
Bake at 425°F/220°C/Gas 7 for 15–20 minutes.

· · · ·

To make mock saffron rice, use ½ teaspoon turmeric and ¼ teaspoon garlic powder for 2 cups uncooked rice. Prepare the rice as usual. It will be the orange-yellow color of saffron and similar in taste.

. . . .

Store open packages of rice in plastic bags and seal well. The rice will remain fresh longer. Aromatic rice, such as basmati, should be stored in the refrigerator.

. . . .

Cooked rice can be stored covered in the refrigerator for up to one week or in the freezer for 2–3 months. To reheat, thaw and place in a saucepan with 2–3 tablespoons water. Simmer covered, until hot, 5–10 minutes. To reheat in microwave, put in correct bowl and cook on high for 3 minutes.

. . . .

A slice of bread can remove the scorched taste from rice. Turn off the heat and place the bread on top of the rice and replace the pot lid and wait a few minutes. The bread will absorb most of the rice's burned aroma. Carefully remove the rice, leaving the burned rice on the bottom of the pot.

. . . .

Stir ¼ cup prepared pesto into 3 cups of hot cooked rice for a delicious gourmet rice.

. . . .

To cook basmati rice, soak it in cold water for 30 minutes, drain, and rinse well. For each cup of rice add 2 cups water, and 1 teaspoon butter or oil may be added. Bring rice and water to a boil for 5 minutes, then cover and simmer until rice has absorbed liquid, about another 5 minutes. Remove from the heat, keep covered, and leave for a few minutes. Uncover and fluff with a fork.

. . . . .

The doneness test for rice and other grains is like the test for pasta, al dente—tender but firm to the bite. At this point, each grain has a slightly resilient core and the cooking liquid has been absorbed.

. . . . .

Use a stock instead of plain water to increase flavor.

. . . . .

If rice is stuck to the bottom of the pan, place the pan in a bowl of cold water and the rice will come away easily.

. . . . .

If the rice is still very chewy or hard in the middle after the allotted time, add just enough water to create a little steam, ¼ cup or less. Put the lid on and cook the rice on very low heat for another 5 minutes.

. . . . .

If the rice is cooked but too wet, uncover the pot and cook over low heat to evaporate the water. Or gently turn the rice out onto a baking sheet and dry it in a low oven.

. . . . .

Soup, Sauce & Gravy

Always make soup at least a day ahead of time, so that the seasonings will have time to improve the flavor. Never use salt or pepper to season soups until near the end of the cooking process as they can intensify and may give the soup too strong a flavor.

. . . .

When cooking soup, always cook with the lid on to help the flavors become better absorbed. Remember that cold soup needs more seasoning than hot soup. The heat tends to drive the flavors into the product more efficiently.

. . . .

Soup bones should be added to the cold water when the soup pot is first placed on the heat. This will allow the maximum release of the flavors, nutrients, and especially the thickening agents.

. . . .

When making soup stock add 1 tablespoon white vinegar to help extract all the calcium from the bones being used. There will be no vinegar taste.

. . . .

To thicken soups or sauces and give a stronger flavor, reduce liquid by cooking with the lid off the saucepan.

. . . .

An excellent thickener for soup is a little oatmeal. It will add flavor and richness to almost any soup.

. . . .

If using wine in soup, do not over-salt. Most wines will increase the saltiness.

. . . . .

For over-salted soup or stew, add one thinly sliced potato per liter while simmering and discard once they have cooked and absorbed the salt. Another remedy is to add cider vinegar and sugar. Gradually add cider vinegar and sugar in ½ teaspoon increments. First add ½ teaspoon sugar, taste, and add ½ teaspoon vinegar if necessary. Repeat if required.

. . . . .

To clarify soup, consommé, or used oil or fats, let them drip through a coffee filter in a funnel.

. . . . .

Remove the fat in soups by adding a lettuce leaf to absorb the fat. Remove the leaf after fat removal. Or toss in a few ice cubes. Stir them around and the fat will stick to the cubes and is easily removed. Place a sheet of waxed paper or plastic wrap directly onto the top of the liquid before refrigerating it. Once it has cooled thoroughly, peel off the waxed paper and the grease will peel off with it.

. . . . .

A few cloves added to vegetable soup will give it a delicious flavor. Put ¼ teaspoon dill seed in a cheesecloth bag and add to potato soup. Add 1–2 bay leaves to tomato soup. Use rice to thicken mushroom soup.

. . . . .

When too much garlic is added to soup or stew, simmer a sprig or small quantity of parsley in it for about 10 minutes.

. . . .

For cream soups, use evaporated skim milk to give a creamy texture with no fat. Or purée leftover rice and add to soup for a creamy texture.

. . . .

Perk up traditional vegetable soup by swirling 2 teaspoons of pesto into each serving bowl.

. . . .

To remove the burned taste from a scorched, cream-based soup or gravy, add a spoonful of smooth peanut butter.

. . . .

Use a fork or wire whisk to stir condensed canned soups.

. . . .

Split peas will not stick to the bottom of the soup pot if a slice of bread is added with the peas to the cooking liquid.

. . . .

Make soups, stock, and gravy in advance and freeze them until required. Use cornstarch as a thickener as ordinary flour can curdle liquids when it is reheated.

. . . .

"A shared meal is food for friendship." —*Unknown*

Avoid using turnips in soups, stews, or stock unless they are used the same day as they are cooked. Turnips go "off" more quickly than other vegetables.

. . . . .

For a convenient single serving, freeze homemade soup in large paper cups.

. . . . .

Quickly chill soups or stews by placing a plastic soda bottle that has been filled with water and frozen into the pot.

. . . . .

Freeze soup in plastic zip bags and freeze flat so that they can stack on top of each other to save space.

. . . . .

Thicken sauces by using the "reduction" method. Boil the liquid so that some of it evaporates. Some recipes recommend the liquid to be reduced by half to give a more concentrated flavor.

. . . . .

Constantly stir roux-thickened sauces while cooking to prevent lumps. If the sauce must be left unattended for a few seconds remove the pan from the heat during that time.

. . . . .

If a roux-thickened sauce develops a few lumps, beat them out with a rotary beater or wire whisk, or strain the sauce.

. . . . .

Cook egg-thickened sauces over low heat or in the top of a double boiler over hot, not boiling, water. Warm the egg yolks before adding to the sauce by stirring a little of the hot sauce mixture into them first. Then add to the remainder of the sauce mixture. Never let a sauce boil after the egg yolks are added as the sauce may curdle. The water must not touch the bottom of the pan holding the sauce.

. . . .

A roux is equal parts unsalted butter and flour, cooked until pale gold in color. The flour in the roux will thicken as its temperature slowly increases. Remove from the heat and when cool, store in a screw top jar in the refrigerator. When making a sauce, use 2 tablespoons of the mixture to ½ pint liquid. Heat the liquid and crumble in the roux, stirring gently but consistently until thickened and smooth. Or spread the mixture out on a tray and cool until firm. Cut into pieces and freeze until required.

. . . .

When making a flour-based sauce the roux must be cooked to remove the flour flavor and must always be hot when added to cold liquids and cold when added to hot for it to work correctly.

. . . .

To prepare white sauce at the right consistency, remember 1-2-3. For each cup of milk use 1 tablespoon flour for a thin sauce, 2 tablespoons flour for a medium sauce, and 3 tablespoons flour for a thick sauce. Use 2 tablespoons butter or margarine for any thickness.

. . . .

Cornstarch and arrowroot have almost twice the thickening power of flour. Cornstarch produces a sauce that is almost clear and shiny or glossy in appearance. Arrowroot has the same qualities and produces a clearer sauce but is more expensive. To use the starches, combine them with a little cold water or wine and stir out any lumps to make a slurry. Add the slurry to a boiling liquid and whisk until the sauce has thickened. If the sauce is allowed to cook too long, the starch will lose some of its thickening capacity.

. . . . .

When making a roux-thickened sauce, make it just a little thin, then finish with cornstarch or arrowroot to give the sauce a glossy look.

. . . . .

Use fine dry breadcrumbs as a thickener for cream sauces or casseroles to give a toasted flavor to the sauce.

. . . . .

When using yogurt in a heated sauce first whisk 2 teaspoons flour into each cup of yogurt to stop it from separating.

. . . . .

Never heat pesto sauce, the basil will turn black and taste bitter.

. . . . .

For a quick vegetable sauce warm a large carton plain yogurt, beat in two egg yolks, and cook stirring constantly for 3 minutes. Season to taste. Pour over the vegetables.

To keep cream sauces from separating, shake the pan in a back-and-forth motion and add a little more cream at the very end to keep the sauce from having an oily texture. This is more successful than stirring with a wire whisk.

. . . .

If a sauce curdles, take the pan immediately off the heat and plunge it into cold water or add 1 teaspoon cold water or a few ice cubes. Whisk well and the sauce will become smooth.

. . . .

To help a curdled mayonnaise, break an egg into a clean bowl and gradually whisk in the curdled mixture.

. . . .

For a steak sauce, after searing steaks, deglaze the frying pan with brandy. Add 2 tablespoons butter, a little white wine, and a splash of Grand Marnier. Or mix equal amounts of ketchup and Worcestershire sauce with a dash of onion powder. Serve over steaks.

. . . .

1 teaspoon vanilla extract added to tomato sauces helps cut the acidity of the tomatoes. Or drop a whole carrot into the sauce while it simmers. Remove the carrot before serving.

. . . .

Use powdered milk in sauces, custards, and baking.

. . . .

Spread a thin layer of melted butter or cream over puddings and other sauces right after cooking. Stir to remove skin.

. . . .

Use the liquid from canned vegetables in soups, sauces, or stews and for making white sauce for creamed vegetables.

. . . . .

White sauce can be used as the base for a variety of sauces. For Veloute sauce use fish stock instead of milk. For onion sauce cook 1 tablespoon minced onion in butter until translucent, add the flour, and continue with the recipe. Mornay sauce has ½ cup of grated swiss, gruyere, or emmental cheese added after the sauce thickens.

. . . . .

Add soy sauce and seasoning to leftover juice from a can of pineapple for a great marinade sauce.

. . . . .

When making pizza sauce, the intensity of the tomato sauce can be adjusted by the amount of crushed peppercorn and garlic used. Adding balsamic vinegar will increase the tang of the sauce.

. . . . .

Chili Sauce: Sauté 2 tablespoons each chopped bell pepper and onion. Add 1¼ cups ketchup and a dash of chili powder.

. . . . .

Barbecue Sauce: Combine ½ cup vinegar, 1 cup ketchup, ½ cup chopped onion, ½ teaspoon cayenne pepper, ½ cup brown sugar, 2 teaspoons dry mustard, 2 tablespoons Worcestershire sauce, ½ cup vegetable oil, and ½ teaspoon salt. Simmer for 30 minutes.

. . . . .

Savory Barbecue Sauce: Combine 1 cup ketchup, ¼ cup lemon juice, ¼ cup butter, ¼ cup packed dark brown sugar, 1 small onion (finely chopped), 1 garlic clove (minced), 2 tablespoons prepared mustard, and 2 tablespoons Worcestershire sauce in a large saucepan. Place over medium heat, bring to a boil, and simmer for 15 minutes until sauce thickens, stirring frequently.

. . . .

Jellied Peach Sauce: This can be used instead of cranberry sauce. Drain 1 large can of peaches, saving the syrup. Purée the peaches in the blender. Add water to the drained syrup to make 1 cup liquid. Pour into a saucepan and add ½ cup sugar and ½ teaspoon nutmeg, bring to a boil, and let boil for 1 minute. Empty a box of lemon gelatin into a bowl and stir in the hot liquid mixture until the gelatin is dissolved. Add puréed peaches and pour into a mold. Chill until set.

. . . .

Applesauce: Place chopped peeled apples in a saucepan with enough water to cover halfway. Cook over medium-low heat, stirring occasionally, until soft. Add lemon juice, sugar, and cinnamon.

. . . .

Tartar Sauce: Combine 2 tablespoons sweet pickle relish or chopped sweet pickles, 4 tablespoons mayonnaise, 1 tablespoon chopped onion, 1 tablespoon chopped hard-boiled egg, a few drops lemon juice, and ½ teaspoon mustard.

. . . .

Teriyaki Sauce: Combine ¼ cup soy sauce, ¼ cup dry sherry, 2 tablespoons brown sugar, ½ teaspoon ground ginger, and ⅛ teaspoon garlic powder.

. . . .

*"Life may be as dull as a cold dinner,
but a little laughter makes a tasty sauce."* —*Unknown*

Curry Sauce: Add 1–3 teaspoons of curry powder (to taste) to the butter and simmer for 1 minute before adding the flour. Continue with the white sauce recipe as directed.

· · · ·

Frozen gravy or sauce may be a little thicker after thawing than when they were freshly made. Add a little appropriate liquid milk, broth, bouillon, or wine to thin them to the desired consistency.

· · · ·

Combine excess fat from a cooked chicken with enough flour to allow it to be rolled into small balls. Freeze on a tray and when frozen transfer to a plastic bag and store frozen. Use to thicken chicken gravy when required.

· · · ·

To make gravy smooth, keep a jar with a mixture of equal parts of flour and cornstarch. Put 3–4 tablespoons of this mixture into a plastic squeeze bottle, add some water, and shake to a smooth paste. Squeeze into the liquid to be thickened, stirring constantly. Or add a pinch of salt to flour before mixing it with water.

· · · ·

To thicken thin gravy, add a little instant mashed potato flakes.

· · · ·

To darken gravy without changing its taste, add 1 teaspoon instant coffee granules. Leftover drip coffee also flavors and darkens gravy. Or to give gravy great color and flavor, add a few teaspoons of soy sauce.

· · · ·

Placing flour in a cup in the oven next to a roast will ensure brown flour for gravy when the meat is done.

. . . .

Use flours that are low in protein and high in starch, such as cake flour, pastry flour, or all-purpose flour. This will help prevent any "skin" from forming on gravy as it sits.

. . . .

To fix lumpy gravy, pour it into a liquidizer and blend 30–60 seconds. Do not over-blend. Pour back into pot and reheat.

. . . .

When gravy is too salty, put in a few pieces of toasted bread for 2–3 minutes to absorb much of the salt.

. . . .

A small amount of baking soda added to gravy will eliminate excess grease.

. . . .

A generous dash of sherry added to gravy creates a rich delicious flavor.

. . . .

When making pork gravy, use ½ beef bouillon cube and ½ teaspoon chicken instant bouillon.

Meat & Poultry

WINE

If a bottle of red wine is cold and you want to drink it right away, remove the foil bottle top and wrap the bottle in a dry kitchen towel. Place in a microwave and heat for 20 seconds, leave to stand for a minute, and repeat the process. Uncork the bottle and allow to breathe for a few minutes.

. . . . .

To chill wine quickly, put the wine bottle in an ice bucket, add a layer of ice, and sprinkle with salt. Repeat until the ice and salt reaches the neck of the bottle. Pour water in until it reaches the height of the ice. The bottle of wine will chill in 10 minutes. Or wet a hand towel and wring it out. Wrap it around the wine bottle and put in the freezer for 10 minutes.

. . . . .

Open red wines an hour before drinking to allow them to breathe. Serve at room temperature. Chill white wines and Rosé, opening just before serving.

. . . . .

Champagne should only be ice-chilled up to the neck of the bottle—any higher and the cork may be difficult to remove.

. . . . .

When not consuming a whole bottle of champagne at once, hang a teaspoon down the open neck of the bottle, put it in the refrigerator, and it will keep its fizz for days.

. . . . .

"Never cook with any wine you wouldn't drink!" —Unknown

Wine is best poured from a height as it airs the wine
and adds aroma.

. . . .

The ideal wineglass should hold around 7 fluid ounces
(200 milliliters) wine and curve inwards at the rim to hold the
scent of the wine. It should never be filled more than ⅓ full. For
estimated servings, allow one glass of wine per guest per hour.
The average serving of dinner wine or champagne is 3–3½ fluid
ounces (75–100 milliliters), for cocktail/dessert wine, 2–2½ fluid
ounces (50–65 milliliters).

. . . .

A dry wine always precedes a sweet one, as the sweet taste will
linger. Sweet wines should be served with desserts.

. . . .

Use a clean stocking as a filter to strain homemade wine.

Freeze leftover wine in ice cube trays and place cubes in a plastic bag when frozen. Use to enhance soups or stews.

· · · ·

To remove an obstinate cork from a bottle, wrap a very hot cloth around the neck of the bottle and the cork should pull out easily.

· · · ·

Have one bottle of dry white wine and one bottle of red wine for both cooking and drinking.

MEAT

To discourage bacterial growth, meat needs to breathe. Remove the plastic wrapper and store in a container in the coldest part of the refrigerator.

· · · ·

When marinating food, remember foods like vegetables or chicken soak up marinades more quickly than pork or red meat. For chicken, shrimp, fish, or vegetables, 3-4 hours is usually long enough to marinate in the refrigerator. With pork or red meat, 6 hours or overnight works the best.

· · · ·

A marinade should completely cover the food, so weigh the food down by placing a plate on top of it. Or marinate food in a plastic bag—the meat stays in the marinade and it is easy to rearrange and turn. Discard the bag when done.

· · · ·

*"Condiments are like old friends—highly thought of,
but often taken for granted." —Unknown*

Marinating meat in vinegar kills bacteria and tenderizes the meat. Use ¼ cup vinegar for a 2–3-pound (1–1.5-kilogram) roast, marinate overnight, and cook without draining or rinsing the meat. Add herbs to the vinegar when marinating as desired.

· · · · ·

Sprinkle a few drops of olive oil on raw meat and leave for an hour before cooking. The meat absorbs the oil and makes it juicier and more tender.

· · · ·

Tough meat can be tenderized by marinating with vinegar or pineapple juice for several hours. The marinade must be washed off to get the taste away though.

· · · ·

When marinating with citrus juice, never leave meat in the marinade for more than 20 minutes. The meat will begin to "cook" in the acid of the juice and will become mushy.

· · · ·

Marinate beef in the refrigerator, never at room temperature.

· · · ·

Marinade that has been in contact with uncooked meat must be boiled before using in a sauce.

· · · ·

Marinate in a food-safe plastic bag or nonreactive container. Turn or stir the meat occasionally to allow even exposure to the marinade. Never save and reuse a marinade.

. . . .

Stew will be tender and tangy if the meat is first marinated in dill pickle juice overnight. Just reduce the salt in the recipe.

. . . .

When preparing a pot roast, use cola instead of water—it tenderizes and gives a unique flavor.

. . . .

Preseason or marinate meat before putting it in the freezer. When defrosted it will be well seasoned. Meats absorb a thin marinade better.

. . . .

Browning meat in oil or melted fat develops flavor, seals in juices, and improves the appearance of the finished dish.

. . . .

Never pierce meats when browning them as the juices will escape and the meats will become tough and dry. Instead, use tongs to turn them over.

. . . .

When browning meat in oil, sometimes the meat sticks to the pan when trying to turn it. If this happens, take the pan off the burner and allow it to sit for a minute or two. The moisture in the food will loosen it from the pan and it can then be turned easily.

. . . .

When browning meat with the bone left in, be careful as the sharp edges can scratch the nonstick surface of a pan.

. . . .

Salt meat after cooking or browning as salt draws moisture out of meats.

. . . .

Salted meats that require boiling should be put in cold water and allowed to heat slowly.

. . . .

To prevent corned beef from turning stringy and dry after cooking, let it cool in the cooking liquid until it is warm rather than hot, then remove and slice for serving.

. . . .

When braising meat, cook at a low temperature for a long time. Add 5–10 milliliters of sugar to improve the flavor, or use 2 cups of hot tea as a cooking liquid.

. . . .

Most casseroles can be made up to 24 hours in advance and refrigerated. Add 15–20 minutes to the cooking time.

. . . .

Sauté meat and vegetables in fruit juice or Worcestershire sauce instead of oil.

. . . .

Use a pastry blender to cut ground beef into small pieces before or after browning.

. . . .

When browning cubes of meat or mince for a casserole, sear meat in a hot pan in small quantities, stirring, over high heat until well browned all over. This will give the dish a rich color and flavor.

. . . .

Burgers and meatballs are juiciest when they are made from regular ground beef, which generally contains the highest percentage of fat. Meatloaves and casseroles are best made with lean or medium ground beef.

. . . .

When burgers or meatballs are made with lean ground beef add finely chopped, sautéed vegetables, herbs, or spices to the mix to make them moist and more flavorsome.

. . . .

Use beaten egg to bind the mixture when making burgers or meatballs.

When making hamburger patties, shape them gently. Over-handling will result in a compact texture after cooking. If grilling, place the patties in the freezer for a few minutes before placing on the grill to help them hold their shape. Never press or flatten with a spatula while cooking.

. . . . .

Hamburgers and meatballs are shaped more easily with wet hands.

. . . . .

Hamburgers should be ¾ inch (18 millimeters) thick and cooked over a slightly lower fire so they do not burn on the outside before being cooked on the inside. Add 1 egg yolk per 1 pound (450 grams) hamburger to help bind the meat.

. . . . .

For a juicier barbecued or grilled hamburger, rub both sides of the meat with cold water before grilling.

. . . . .

Extend 1 pound (450 grams) ground meat for meatballs or hamburgers with ½ cup cottage cheese. It increases flavor and servings.

. . . . .

For extra juicy hamburgers add ¼ cup evaporated milk to every 1 pound (450 grams) of meat being used.

. . . . .

Poke a hole in the middle of hamburgers while shaping them. The burgers will cook faster and the holes will disappear when done.

. . . . .

To cook a large number of hamburgers, line a large roasting pan with heavy-duty foil and place a layer of burgers on it. Put a second layer of foil over them and add another layer of burgers. Repeat as necessary up to four layers, then top with foil. Bake 35 minutes at 350°F/180°C/Gas 6. If preferred, cook the meat for 20 minutes and then finish cooking burgers on a grill.

. . . . .

Before freezing ground beef, flatten it into a square or patties rather than leaving it in a mound. It will thaw faster later.

. . . . .

Meatballs can be bound with grated apple or potato instead of egg.

. . . . .

When making meatballs, place the meat mixture in the refrigerator for 30 minutes first. They will be easier to form and will not fall apart when cooking.

. . . . .

To make meatballs of equal size, form the meat into a 1-inch (2.5-centimeter) thick rectangle. Cut the rectangle into an equal number of squares and roll into balls.

. . . . .

A fast way to make meatballs is to shape the meat mixture into a log and cut off slices. The slices roll easily into balls.

. . . .

Use a gentle touch with ground beef. Overmixing or compacting will result in dense burgers, meatballs, or meatloaves when cooked.

. . . .

To avoid greasy, raw meatballs put them in a pot of boiling water and cook until browned. Strain in a colander before using in a recipe.

. . . .

When making meatloaf, first combine all ingredients except the ground beef to evenly distribute the seasoning.

. . . .

Combine all the ingredients for a meatloaf in a plastic bag, remove all air, seal, and knead the bag to blend. Or use a potato masher to combine ingredients.

. . . .

When making a meatloaf, handle the meat as little as possible. When shaping and placing into the loaf pan, do not press down to compact meat.

. . . .

Before adding chopped onions or celery to meatloaf, sauté in butter, margarine, or salad oil. This enhances the flavor.

. . . .

Stretch a meatloaf by adding oatmeal, cooked rice, or other quick cooking or precooked grains or vegetables.

. . . .

Meatloaf will not stick to the pan if a strip of bacon is placed on the bottom of the pan before adding the meatloaf ingredients to it.

. . . .

Brush cold water over the top of a meatloaf to prevent it from cracking.

. . . .

Bake meatloaf in muffin tins for individual servings.

. . . .

Meatloaf doesn't have to be a loaf! Try baking one in a ring mold, then fill the center with green peas, beans or other vegetables, creamed mushrooms, or mashed potatoes.

. . . .

As a change from a potato topping on a shepherd's pie, butter slices of white bread, cut into small squares, and arrange on top of the meat and vegetables. Sprinkle grated cheese over and bake as usual.

. . . .

Add 1 tablespoon horseradish to the potato topping of a shepherd's pie and sprinkle cheese on top.

. . . .

Put a pinch of baking soda in spaghetti sauce to remove the acid taste from the tomatoes.

. . . .

For successful grilling of beef, select the right cut. Always look for steaks with marbling which is the inter-muscular fat running through the meat, giving it flavor.

. . . .

To prevent spattering when pan-frying meats, first sprinkle a little salt into the pan.

. . . .

Chefs pound meat not to tenderize the meat but to help level the meat so it cooks evenly.

. . . .

To fry steak, preheat a heavy skillet until very hot. Sprinkle a thin layer of salt over the bottom of the pan; sear steak quickly to seal in juices, then cook to desired doneness.

. . . .

Rub the steak well with oil before grilling. The heat will char the oil not the steak and seal in the juices.

. . . .

When grilling meat, place a few pieces of dry bread in the grill pan to soak up dripping fat. This helps to eliminate smoking fat and reduces the chance that it could alight.

. . . .

Cut slits in the fat all the way around the meat before cooking to stop it curling.

· · · · ·

When cooking on the grill, use apple juice in a spray bottle to baste the meat. This enhances the flavor and prevents the meat from drying out.

· · · · ·

Do not turn the beef during the first few minutes of grilling so that a coating can form to protect the food and retain the natural juices.

· · · · ·

To cook steak on the grill, cook on one side until beads appear on top, then turn and cook a further minute. Do not turn again nor press the steak with the spatula.

· · · · ·

Experienced cooks can poke a piece of meat and know if it is rare, medium, or well done, since all proteins are firm when heated. Rare meat feels like the part of the hand where the thumb and forefinger meet, soft but slightly firm. Close the hand into a loose fist, poke the same spot and it resembles the texture of medium meat; a tight fist is like well done.

· · · · ·

To pan roast tender cuts of meat, chicken, or fish, use a heavy-bottomed ovenproof pan. Heat the pan on top of a medium-high burner, add a little oil and heat until it is almost smoking, then sear the food. Finish cooking in a hot oven. The timing depends on what is being cooked.

· · · · ·

Never cut into steaks, chops, or chicken breasts when they are in the pot or frying pan. Transfer them on to a plate and then cut through the food.

· · · · ·

Fresh meats and poultry can be left in the original store wrapping when freezing for less than two weeks. For longer freezer storage, over-wrap with a suitable freezer wrap.

· · · · ·

Breaded meat and fish hold their coatings better if the crumbs are mixed with flour.

· · · · ·

To prevent crumbs from falling off steaks and chops in the frying pan, bread them several hours before using and place in refrigerator.

· · · · ·

A standard portion of meat is 3 ounces (75 grams), about the size of a deck of cards. Most people eat at least twice that.

· · · · ·

A shallow pan is better for roasting meats because it allows heat to circulate around the roast.

· · · · ·

When roasting beef, place it in the pan fat-side up. This allows the fat to self-baste the meat, ensuring a moist and tender roast.

· · · · ·

A roast with the bone in will cook faster than a boneless roast—the bone carries the heat to the inside of the roast.

· · · · ·

At the beginning of cooking, insert a meat thermometer into the meat as near to the center as possible, avoiding bone and fatty areas. Leave in until the meat reaches the desired temperature.

· · · · ·

When roasting a joint of lamb or beef, put ½ pint (300 milliliters) cold water into the baking tray. This reduces shrinkage, keeps the meat succulent, and gives stock for the gravy.

· · · · ·

To reheat roast, wrap in aluminum foil and heat in a slow oven.

· · · · ·

If roast beef is scorched, cut off the burned edges, cover with apricot jam, or soak the meat briefly in milk to remove the burned aftertaste.

· · · · ·

A roast will stay hot for an hour if it is wrapped in doubled aluminum foil and then in several thicknesses of newspaper.

Allow a roast to stand for 15 minutes after removing it from the oven. This will ease slicing.

· · · · ·

Use moist heat methods such as braising, simmering, stewing, or poaching to cook less tender cuts of beef. Moist heat and long, slow simmering in a tightly covered pan results in tender meat. Moist heat means gently simmering, not boiling, which keeps the meat from shrinkage and keeps it moist and juicy.

· · · · ·

To prevent leftover meat from becoming dry and tough when reheating, place lettuce leaves between slices.

· · · · ·

If a roast is undercooked, slice the meat onto a heatproof platter and return it to the oven until it is done as required.

· · · · ·

To carve a leg of lamb, set the roast on a platter with the shank bone to carver's right. Cut lengthways slices from the thin side. Turn leg over so it rests on the cut side. Make vertical slices down to leg bone. Cut horizontally along bone to release slices.

· · · · ·

Older lamb can sometimes taste of mutton. To improve the flavor, wipe the surface with a clean, damp cloth, brushing it with equal parts of lemon juice and olive oil. Allow to marinate for 2 hours before roasting with a sprinkle of garlic.

· · · · ·

Use lemon juice to bind stuffing for pork, chicken, or meat dishes to give a different flavor.

. . . .

The tenderest pork chops are those with pink rather than red meat. For tastier pork chops sprinkle them with soy sauce when grilling or barbecuing.

. . . .

Rub baking soda into the fat surrounding pork chops to make them extra crispy.

. . . .

For speedy barbecued ribs, cut the slabs of ribs into halves or thirds. Cover and microwave on high for 10 minutes, rearranging the pieces after 5 minutes. Place on the grill and brush with barbecue sauce. Grill until cooked, turning and brushing occasionally with additional barbecue sauce.

. . . .

To bake a moist ham, empty a can of cola into the baking pan, wrap the ham in aluminum foil, and bake. Thirty minutes before the ham is finished, remove the foil, allowing the drippings to mix with the cola for a lovely brown gravy.

. . . .

Add 1 tablespoon (15 milliliters) vinegar and 1 teaspoon (5 milliliters) sugar to the water when cooking a bacon joint. Leave to cool in the liquor.

. . . .

Before opening a package of bacon, roll it. This helps separate the slices for easy removal of individual slices.

. . . . .

Wrap bacon in foil instead of plastic wrap. Bacon will stay fresher for longer this way.

. . . . .

To stop bacon rashers curling during cooking, dip them in cold water before frying. Start cooking bacon rashers in a cold pan and cook slowly.

. . . . .

Dust bacon slices with flour to stop them burning. Mixing sugar with flour gives a sugar-cured flavor.

. . . . .

Spread raw bacon rashers on a baking sheet to freeze them and extend their keeping time. Once they are solid, they can be stored in a plastic bag in the freezer. Or fry all the rashers, drain off the fat, and store the strips in a freezer container until needed. No need to thaw before reheating.

. . . . .

Instead of frying bacon, bake it in an oven on a baking tray at 350°F/180°C/Gas 4 for 15–20 minutes, depending how crisp the bacon is desired.

. . . . .

When a recipe calls for crumbled bacon, dice it before frying for more even cooking.

. . . . .

Soak salty rashers in warm water for 15 minutes or soak in milk for 5 minutes and then dry well before grilling or frying. Sprinkle a little sugar on salty bacon before cooking, removing any surplus before frying.

· · · ·

To separate frozen bacon rashes, heat a metal spatula in boiling water and then slide in between the bacon slices.

· · · ·

Sausage skins will peel off easily if they are held under a cold running tap for a minute.

· · · ·

Sausages or sausage patties rolled in flour before frying will shrink less or crack open during cooking.

· · · ·

Before cooking sausages on the grill, put them in a pot and cover with cold water. Bring to a boil, remove from the water, and cool under the cold tap. Dry thoroughly before cooking.

· · · ·

A tasty variation for hot dogs is to add mashed potato to rolls or pita bread with the frankfurter and tomato sauce or mustard, then crisp them in a hot oven.

· · · ·

Venison is one of the lowest fat, lowest cholesterol, healthiest meats. To remove the wild taste, soak venison in lightly salted water overnight. Use the same cooking times and temperatures for venison as for beef.

. . . .

Veal is a delicately flavored meat. Seasonings that enhance veal's natural flavors include white wine, sherry, onion, celery, parsley, butter, marjoram, rosemary, sage, oregano, black pepper, cinnamon, garlic, mustard, nutmeg, bay leaf, and thyme.

. . . .

Coat veal cutlets with crushed cheese biscuit crumbs instead of breadcrumbs for a different flavor.

. . . .

If a stew or soup saucepan is burned, pour everything but the burned scrapings into a fresh pot. Add a few onions or a few drops of lemon juice to help neutralize the scorched flavor.

. . . .

For thicker and richer stews, before serving, add instant potato flakes ¼ cup at a time until gravy is just right.

. . . .

If too much liquid is added to a stew and there is not time to reduce by simmering, add ¼ cup instant oatmeal. It absorbs some of the liquid, making it thicker.

. . . .

Although many people avoid eating the fat on meat it is needed there for cooking. Without some fat, the meat will dry out and lose its flavor when cooked.

. . . . .

Enrich the flavor of a spicy meat casserole with a few pieces of plain or dark chocolate.

. . . . .

Instead of a pastry lid on a pie, try a vegetable topping. Grate a raw carrot, raw parsnip, and a little raw turnip, add 2 cups cold mashed potato, 2 tablespoons (30 milliliters) of melted butter and seasoning to taste. Combine well and use to cover the pie. Bake for one hour in a moderate oven.

. . . . .

When putting a pastry lid on meat or fish pies, place a heatproof eggcup in the center of the filling to keep the lid up when the filling decreases during cooking.

. . . . .

Stock is tastier if meat bones and vegetables are soaked for an hour in cold water before bringing to a boil. Always start a meat stock in cold water to pull the most juices from the meat. Clarify stock by simmering a few eggshells in it.

. . . . .

To avoid risk of bacterial growth, do not leave prepared stock in the refrigerator longer than 2 days. Freeze for longer storage.

Do not freeze stocks longer than six months. Poultry and veal stocks begin to lose their flavor and fish stocks will give a very strong smell.

. . . .

Never use internal organs such as livers, hearts, gizzards, or kidneys in making stock. They contain blood that gives stock a very strong and unpleasant taste.

. . . .

To improve the flavor of canned bouillon and consommé, try simmering with some additional seasonings such as extra onion, garlic, celery, and/or bouquet garni for 5 minutes to improve the flavor.

POULTRY

The color of chicken skin does not indicate quality. Skin color ranges from yellow to white, depending on the breed of chicken and what it was fed.

. . . .

When a surplus amount of chicken is purchased, boil it and take the meat from the bones, package, and freeze in cup-sized portions and use as required.

. . . .

When estimating the amount of poultry needed, the rule of thumb for turkey is 1 pound (450 grams) raw weight per person. With chicken plan on ½ pound (225 grams) bone-in weight per person. One half breast or two drumsticks or four wings are considered a serving. With skinless, boneless chicken breasts use one per person depending on size.

. . . .

Use ½–¾ cup of stuffing per 1 pound (450 grams) turkey and stuff the neck cavity loosely. Never stuff a turkey ahead of time as bacterial growth can contaminate the stuffing. Stuff the bird just before roasting it.

. . . . .

Raw poultry is highly perishable and should be stored in the coldest part of the refrigerator for no longer than 2 days.

. . . . .

Frozen poultry should be thawed in the refrigerator, not at room temperature. It can also be defrosted under cold running water. The water should be changed frequently.

. . . . .

To remove pinfeathers easily, rub the skin with salt first.

. . . . .

Rub raw chicken with a clean, dry terry washcloth and the skin will pull right off. Or use a paper towel to hold on to the skin and pull firmly.

. . . . .

Chicken will have a crisper skin if a small amount of mayonnaise is rubbed over it before roasting.

. . . . .

When breading chicken or chops add 1 tablespoon mustard to the breading mixture.

. . . . .

Enhance the flavor of poultry by massaging marjoram into the skin before cooking. For a freezer-burned bird or if the skin looks dry, rub olive oil into the skin.

· · · · ·

Reduce a wild bird's game flavor by rubbing sherry, brandy, or powdered ginger into its skin before roasting. Add a dash of any one of these to the gravy, too.

· · · · ·

When not stuffing poultry, prick the skin of a whole lemon and place it in the cavity. Placing a cup of water in the cavity also bastes the bird. Or put a large knob of butter mashed with 1 tablespoon dried tarragon into the cavity and baste the bird with the juices during cooking.

· · · · ·

Always roast poultry breast-side down so the white meat will not dry out. Turn the bird over during the final 20 minutes of cooking to brown the breast skin.

· · · · ·

Poultry should be roasted at 325°F/160°C/Gas 3 or higher to avoid potential food safety problems. Check that the bird is fully cooked with a thermometer or slit the thickest part to observe the color. When fully cooked it is no longer pink.

· · · · ·

To check if poultry is completely cooked, try flexing the legs from side to side. If they "give" easily then it is ready.

· · · · ·

Rescue dried-out poultry by slicing the meat onto a heatproof platter. Combine equal amounts of poultry broth and butter sauce and ladle over the meat. Let the bird baste in this juice in an oven 250°F/125°C/Gas ½ for 10 minutes. Or cut the meat into chunks and add to a savory sauce.

. . . .

Poultry is easily moved from pan to platter by using a pair of clean rubber gloves. They will improve the grip and insulate hands from the heat of the bird.

. . . .

When making chicken strips, use frozen boneless chicken breasts, defrosted for 30 minutes.

. . . .

To flatten chicken breasts or other meats, use a heavy frying pan. Or place chicken breasts between pieces of plastic wrap or waxed paper and, using heel of the hand, apply firm pressure, pounding lightly, until they are the required thickness.

. . . .

For crispy fried chicken, coat with half flour and half cornstarch, season as usual, and add ½ teaspoon baking powder.

. . . .

To easily flour meat or chicken pieces, shake them, a few at a time, in a bag with the seasoned flour or crumbs. Shake off any excess coating. Leave in the refrigerator for 1 hour before cooking.

. . . .

When breading chicken breasts, brush mayonnaise onto the meat and sprinkle on breadcrumbs. The mayonnaise keeps the meat moist.

· · · ·

To fry chicken pieces, melt a little sour cream in a pan and brown the meat. Pour 1 cup sour cream over it and cook in a moderate oven for 1 hour. Remove the chicken and make gravy with the drippings.

Fruits of the Sea

FISH SPECIES

Bass—round fish with delicate flesh.

Bream—sea bream is a round fish with coarse scales.

Brill—firm white, flat fish that looks likes turbot.

Cod—round fish with close white flesh and mild flavor.

Coley—like cod but has grayish raw flesh that cooks white.

Conger Eel—oily fish with a distinctive flavor.

Dogfish—firm-fleshed member of the shark family.

Dover Sole—flat fish, white, textured flesh, good flavor.

Flounder—flat fish similar to plaice with white, soft flesh.

Haddock—like cod with firm, fine-textured white flesh.

Hake—round white fish, member of the cod family.

Halibut—large, flat fish, with creamy flesh.

Herring—oily fish with lots of bones but very tasty.

John Dory—oval, flat body, spiny head, delicate flesh.

Lemon sole—flat white fish like plaice.

Mackerel—oily fish, must be eaten when very fresh.

Monkfish—firm-textured, mild, sweet flavor like lobster.

Pike—large oily fish, coarse flesh.

Pilchard—large sardine, generally sold canned.

Plaice—flat fish, soft, sweet flesh.

Red Mullet—red skin, creamy white flesh, needs scaling.

Red Snapper—firm white flesh, large flakes, mild taste.

Rockfish—known as cat fish, firm pinkish-colored flesh.

Sardine—small oily fish, can be fresh or canned.

Skate—flat fish with large "wings," which is the part to eat.

Trout—rainbow or brown variety, oily fish, creamy flesh.

Trout—sea trout, pink flesh, similar to salmon in flavor.

Salmon—oily fish, pink flesh, flaky texture.

Shark—flesh is dense and meat-like, ammonia smell.

Swordfish—mild-flavored, firm, dense, meat-like flesh.

Tuna—oily, rich-flavored flesh, firmly textured, flaky.
Turbot—large flat fish with creamy flavor.
Whitebait—oily fish, like very small herring.
Whiting—round fish like cod, more bony, soft flaky flesh.

To distinguish some common species

Plaice has grayish upper side with bright orange spots and a white underside.
Haddock has a dark lateral line along the skin surface.
Skinless cod fillets have a distinctive white papery membrane along the belly and a white line of fat along the lateral line of the fillet.
Shark and swordfish look alike, but shark has a dark streak of flesh in the center and rough skin along the edge.
Red Snapper has lustrous pink scales.

CHOWDER

Basic chowder starts with bacon, onions, celery, a roux, or equal amounts of cornstarch and flour or instant potatoes, milk and/or cream.

· · · · ·

Add roux to the milk or cream at the beginning of cooking to prevent the chowder from curdling and separating.

· · · · ·

Use powdered milk in chowder that is to be frozen and it will not break down when thawing.

· · · · ·

When making thick chowder, just before serving, add a stick of butter and stir it in until it finishes melting. This will give a rich, buttery-tasting chowder.

. . . .

Use waxy potatoes in chowder, as they do not go mushy.

. . . .

For rich, flavorful chowder, use cream instead of milk.

. . . .

Save the shells from shrimp and lobster and cook in water for 20 minutes, strain, and use as fish stock for chowder.

. . . .

The basis for good chowder is a good fish stock. To make a fish stock combine 10 pounds (4 kilograms) fish bones and trimmings, 10 pints (6 liters) water, 2 chopped onions, 1 small bunch chopped celery, 2–3 bay leaves, 1 bunch parsley, and 1 pound (450 grams) chopped mushrooms in a large saucepan. Bring to a simmer, reduce heat, and cook 30–40 minutes. Skim surface as required. Remove from heat and strain through a fine sieve, discarding vegetables. Add 2 cups white wine for a different flavor.

. . . .

When making stock, always add cold water to fish or meat and bones. Hot water forces the release of proteins that cause the stock to become cloudy.

. . . .

Never allow stock to boil. The foam or scum that appears will roll back into the stock when boiling. Always bring stock to a strong simmer so the scum can be skimmed off.

. . . .

Do not use too much water or liquid. The higher the proportion of bone to liquid creates a more flavorful stock.

. . . .

When straining, do not move contents of stock by stirring. When stirred, the stock becomes cloudy.

. . . .

It takes twice as much milk to give the chowder the same texture as cream and this extra milk will water down the flavors of the other ingredients.

. . . .

Store stocks carefully. Warm stock can breed bacteria. Cool and store in refrigerator for a day or in freezer for up to 3 months.

FISH

Smell fish before purchase. It should smell fresh and mild, with no strong fish smell. If the head is present on the fish, the eyes should be clear and bulging, the gills reddish, and the scales very shiny. With fillets or steaks the flesh should be shiny and firm and spring back if pressed with a finger.

. . . .

Cod, haddock, pollock, and hake improve with age. Freshly caught, they taste watery and starchy, but with 3–9 days' refrigeration they develop a sweet and creamy flavor.

. . . . .

Mackerel, tuna, trout, and salmon are all of the same family and can be substituted one for the other when called for in salads, loaves, or casseroles.

. . . . .

Soak fish in salt water or rub well with vinegar before descaling and the scales will come off more easily.

. . . . .

Scale fish fast by aiming the full blast of a hose against the scales, or scrape them off with a plastic mesh pot scrubber or the edge of a sturdy plastic lid. Work underwater and it will not make a mess.

. . . . .

To scale a fish, grip it firmly by the tail. Using a vegetable peeler use short, firm strokes from tail to head to remove the scales.

. . . . .

It is recommended that fish or seafood is cooked on the day of purchase, but sometimes this is not possible. To regain freshness and texture in seafood, soak in cold salted water, occasionally massaging the seafood. Rinse and drain well before proceeding with recipe.

. . . . .

"Fish, to taste right, must swim three times—
in water, in butter, and in wine." —Polish Proverb

To keep fresh fish very cold, place the pieces in a single layer in a baking dish lined with paper towels. Cover the dish tightly with plastic wrap; refrigerate the fish and use as soon as possible.

. . . . .

Defrosting fish should always be achieved slowly in the refrigerator to minimize bacterial contamination. Do not defrost fish in water as the salt-based flavor will be dissolved. Thaw fish in milk for fresher flavor.

. . . . .

Only defrost fish in the microwave if it is to be cooked within 10 minutes of defrosting. The fish should be no more than 1 inch (2.5 centimeters) thick, as it can partially cook and dry out.

. . . . .

If fish smells a little "fishy," place it in a shallow dish and add enough milk blended with 1–2 tablespoons fresh lemon juice to cover. Cover tightly and refrigerate for 1 hour. Do not leave the fish in the milk bath for longer than an hour or it will tend to fall apart when cooked. Drain fish, pat dry on paper towels, and use as desired. This can often salvage fish that has been kept a bit too long before using.

. . . . .

Fish can be deboned before or after cooking. The bones separate quite easily after cooking, but it is often more pleasant to eat fish when the bones have been removed.

. . . . .

Always gut fish and rinse in clean water before deboning. To do so, place the cleaned and dressed fish on a cutting surface. Hold the fish by the head (if the head is still attached) and slice into the fish behind the gill until you feel the knife touch backbone. Turn the knife so it is flat against the backbone, touching the ribs. The edge should face the tail. Cut along the backbone through the fish from head to tail, under the fillet. Turn fish over and repeat. At this point, two sets of bones will remain in the fillet. Cut away the rib cage bones, which will be visible, by sliding the edge of the knife between the rib bones and the meat of the fillet. Lay the fillet, bone side up, across an inverted mixing bowl. The curve of the bowl will cause the bones to stick out, making them easy to find. Use your finger to feel for the pin bone tips sticking out of the fillet and pull them out with tweezers or needle-nose pliers.

· · · ·

Fillet flatfish by making a cut down the backbone (feel for it with fingers first). On either side of the backbone, cut down until you feel the ribs, then slice under the fillet along the ribs until you reach the edge of the fish and the fillets are removed in two pieces per side.

· · · ·

The sharper the knife, the better. Fish flesh is usually very delicate. Do not use serrated or electric knives.

Fish can be sautéed, grilled, broiled, poached, or baked.

. . . .

Before cooking any fresh fish, rinse completely in cold running water and pat dry.

. . . .

Marinate fish fillets in lemon or lime and a little salt before cooking for firmer flesh, easier handling, and a fresh taste.

. . . .

Rub a little mustard on fish fillets before cooking them; it makes the fish taste fresher and less fishy.

. . . .

When shallow frying fish, always coat in seasoned flour or egg as it holds the fish together and keeps it moist.

. . . .

When frying fish, put salt or a dash of vinegar into the pan with oil to prevent sticking and control odor.

. . . .

When frying fish, put fish into the pan skin-side down first, and it will not curl.

. . . .

Poach fish in lemon-seasoned liquid. Fish covered with lettuce leaves will not dry out as it bakes.

. . . .

"Fish should smell like the ocean.
If they smell like fish, it's too late." —*Unknown*

For baking or grilling fish, measure the thickness of the fish at the thickest part. If the fish is stuffed or rolled, measure it after stuffing or rolling and cook 10 minutes for every 1 inch (2.5 centimeters) measured, turning the fish halfway through the cooking time. Pieces of fish less than ½ inch (1 centimeter) thick do not have to be turned over.

. . . . .

Add 5 minutes to the total cooking time if cooking the fish in foil or if the fish is cooked in a sauce. Double the cooking time, 20 minutes per 1 inch (2 centimeters) for frozen fish that has not been defrosted. For baking, oven temperature should be 400°F/200°C/Gas 6.

. . . . .

Eliminate the odor from baking or boiling salmon by squeezing lemon juice on the cut surface of the salmon and leaving it in the refrigerator for 1 hour before cooking.

. . . . .

Fish is completely cooked when the flesh becomes opaque and flakes easily with a fork.

. . . . .

To eliminate fish odor, rub lemon or mustard on cutting boards and utensils.

. . . . .

Any fish canned in oil tastes fresher if it is soaked in fresh oil 30 minutes before serving. Pour off the oil before eating.

. . . .

Water-canned fish benefits from being refreshed in fresh water.

. . . .

Anchovies are less salty if they are soaked in cold water or milk 10–15 minutes before serving. Pat dry with a paper towel.

SHELLFISH

There are many varieties of prawns or shrimp, many of them from warm foreign waters where they grow fast and often large. Scampi is the Italian name for what are called Dublin Bay prawns; these are not in fact prawns at all but a tiny member of the lobster family.

. . . .

The old rule for shellfish generally holds that any month containing the letter R is a good month for shellfish. These are the colder winter months and shellfish prefer cold water. More importantly, warmer waters mean an increase in bacteria levels and the shellfish can be dangerous to eat.

. . . .

When buying shrimp, select ones with the shells closely fitted to the body. Loose shells are a sign of shrinkage and are probably not fresh.

. . . .

"The world may be your oyster,
but you've got to crack the shell yourself." —Unknown

Shrimps that have been peeled and deveined before freezing lose their flavor and texture.

. . . . .

Preparing shrimp is quite simple, but time consuming. Run them under cold water to remove any extra debris and to rinse off any juices. Place the shrimp on a cutting board and remove the head just behind the "helmet."

. . . . .

Hold the fan end of the tail and give it a slight twist to release the meat but not break it off. Holding the tail by the narrow part, unwind the shell starting at the widest part and pulling when you get to the tail to remove the shell.

. . . . .

At the back of the shrimp, if there is a definite grey/black vein, use a paring knife to make a shallow slit in the back and grasp the vein to pull it out. Do not make the cut too deep or the shrimp will "butterfly" when cooking.

. . . . .

Devein an uncooked prawn by inserting a fine skewer just behind the head to draw out the vein in one piece.

. . . . .

Rinse the shrimps to wash off any shell pieces. If not using the shrimp immediately, store them in the refrigerator for up to 2 days in a tightly sealed container.

. . . . .

Add a few drops of sesame oil to the water when cooking shrimp to eliminate the odor.

. . . .

Raw shrimp turn pink and firm when cooked. Depending on the size, it takes from 3–5 minutes to boil or steam 1 pound (450 grams) medium-size shrimp in the shell.

. . . .

Watch shrimp closely for doneness when cooking. If they form a half-circle, they are done and if they have coiled into a circle, they are overdone.

. . . .

Improve the taste of canned shrimp by rinsing well with cold water then soaking in a little sherry and 2 tablespoons vinegar or in wine for 15 minutes before using.

. . . .

The sea scallop is the largest of the scallops; they can be bought fresh or frozen. Scallops freeze well. The raw meat is translucent and shiny in appearance and has a distinct, sweet odor when fresh.

. . . .

Scallops come in decorative shells; the fish itself sits on a flat fan-shaped shell and is enclosed by a similar concave one. Large king scallops with their bright orange coral attached cook very quickly; the corals take only a few seconds, so they are usually removed and added to the pan shortly before serving.

. . . .

Fresh oysters should be closed tight. Do not buy oysters with broken or damaged shells.

. . . . .

Store oysters flat-side up to keep them bathed in their own liquor and refrigerate between 34–40°F but not directly on ice. Keep oysters dry and they can stay alive for 7–10 days.

. . . . .

Oysters are available seasonally. Live oysters need to breathe. Never store them in airtight bags or containers, where they could freeze or where temperatures will fluctuate widely, in a warm place or submerged in ice water or fresh water. Place live oysters in a bowl with a damp towel over it and keep refrigerated.

. . . . .

Frozen oysters on the half shell and meats should always be thawed slowly under refrigeration for 24 hours.

. . . . .

Oyster meats should be plump and have a fresh, mild, saltwater odor. The meat is usually tan and creamy but the color can vary depending on the animal's diet. Green and reddish pigmentation is harmless and the colors disappear during cooking. If the meat is dry or has a pink color and off-odor, it indicates the presence of yeast. Discard it.

. . . . .

Purchase a good oyster knife. Look for one with a thick, solid handle made of sturdy wood or plastic, a finger-guard, and a short, thick, inflexible, pointed blade. Strength and durability will be more important than sharpness or size.

. . . . .

Oysters have very sharp shells so protect the hands with a pair of gardening gloves with rubber palms.

. . . .

Scrub each oyster under running water with a kitchen scrubber.

. . . .

Using a thick kitchen towel, grip the oyster, flat-side up, and force the tip of an oyster knife blade between the shells just next to the hinge. Pry, twisting the knife, while at the same time trying to push the blade into the oyster, breaking the hinge. Try to keep the oyster level so that the liquid inside does not spill out. Run the blade along the inside of the upper shell to free the oyster, removing the top shell. Then scrape along the lower shell and remove the oyster. If serving it on the half shell, pick out any loose fragments from the shell and avoid spilling the oysters' delicious liquid.

. . . .

A beer can opener can be used to open oysters. Wedge the point under the hinge at the top of the oyster, then push down hard.

. . . .

If oysters are soaked in club soda for 5 minutes, they usually come out of their shells more easily.

Clams and oysters will be easier to open if washed with cold water, then placed in a plastic bag and put in the freezer for an hour.

. . . . .

When storing shucked oysters for a couple of days, cover them in their liquor in a closed container set in crushed ice.

. . . . .

When buying mussels, allow at least 1 pint (600 milliliters) per person for a first course, and 1½–2 pints (about 1 liter) for a main course. That may seem a lot, but some will have to be discarded and when they have been shelled, mussels are very small and light.

. . . . .

Although mussels are often thought to be dangerous to eat, mussel poisoning is in fact quite rare. However, it is imperative that they are purchased fresh and checked thoroughly.

. . . . .

Examine mussels carefully before using. If one has a sloshing sound or it feels heavier than it should be, then discard it as it may be filled with sand and dirt.

. . . . .

When purchasing mussels, make sure that they are live. To do this, select mussels that are all tightly closed and not slimy. If it appears that the mussel is even slightly opened, leave it.

. . . . .

Rinse the mussels under cold running water. Remove any loose debris or sand and remove the beard from between the shells.

. . . . .

Steep live mussels in the refrigerator in a bucket of water with 2–3 teaspoons dry mustard or a handful of oatmeal added for a few hours to help remove the grit and sand. Rinse well.

. . . .

Soak mussels for 15–20 minutes in salted water, drain off the water, rinse the mussels, and repeat. Complete the process a total of 3 times. This process will help clean any unwanted sand and debris from inside the shells.

. . . .

Clean mussels by scrubbing, remove the beards and barnacles with a knife, and rinsing several times in cold water. Any mussels that float should be discarded along with any with cracked shells. Mussels with open shells should be tapped and if they do not close these should be discarded.

. . . .

Mussels should open during cooking but they should be stirred as they may have trouble opening if they are too packed together.

. . . .

To remove grit from the cooking liquor, sieve through muslin.

. . . .

Calculate the approximate age of a lobster by multiplying its weight by 4 and then adding 3 years.

. . . .

When storing live lobsters until ready to use, place them in the refrigerator, but not directly on ice.

. . . .

Defrost frozen lobster tails in the refrigerator for 2–3 hours. To speedily defrost, place the lobster, in its sealed package, in a large bowl or pot. Place the pot in the sink and fill with cold water. Let the cold tap trickle into the pot; this will keep the water moving and will assist in the thawing process. Check after 15–20 minutes. Remove from the packaging and they are ready for cooking.

· · · · ·

Boiled lobster turns bright red. Allow 5–6 minutes per 1 pound (450 grams) from when the water returns to a full boil.

· · · · ·

The male crab has more white meat as it has bigger claws. The female crab has the bigger body and more dark meat.

· · · · ·

A crab full of meat should feel heavy for its size. From a crab weighing 1 pound (450 grams) the meat yield should be around 7 ounces (200 grams); from a large 2-pound (900-gram) crab, expect about 12 ounces (350 grams) of meat. When served with some homemade mayonnaise and a salad, 7–8 ounces (200–225 grams) of crabmeat is sufficient for two people as a main course or between four as a starter.

· · · · ·

To remove meat from a crab claw, tap joint with a knife and separate the two halves. Use the handle of a teaspoon to scoop out the meat from inside the claw. Hit the nipper end sharply a couple of times and the outer shell will slide off easily.

· · · · ·

Extend a crab salad with cooked, shredded halibut.

GENERAL SHELF LIVES FOR COMMON ITEMS

Flour, unopened: up to 12 months. Opened: 6–8 months.

Whole Wheat Flour, unopened: 1 month. Opened: 6–8 months if refrigerated.

Sugar, unopened: 2 years. Sugars do not spoil but eventually may change flavor.

Brown sugar, unopened: 4 months.

Powdered sugar, unopened: 18 months.

Solid shortening, unopened: 8 months. Opened: 3 months.

Cocoa, unopened: indefinitely. Opened: 1 year.

Whole spices: 2–4 years, both unopened and open.

Ground spices: 2–3 years, both unopened and open.

Paprika, red pepper, and chili powder: 2 years in refrigerator.

High-acid canned items such as fruit juice, tomato soup, and vinegar, unopened: 12–18 months.

Baking soda, unopened: 18 months. Opened: 6 months.

Baking powder, unopened: 6 months. Opened: 3 months.

Cornstarch: 18 months, both unopened and open.

Dry pasta made without eggs, unopened: 2 years. Opened: 1 year.

Dry egg noodles, unopened: 2 years. Opened: 1–2 months.

Salad dressing, unopened: 10–12 months. Opened: 3 months if refrigerated.

Low-acid canned items such as soup, meats, gravy, and vegetables, unopened: 2–5 years.

Honey: 1 year, both unopened and open.

Worcestershire sauce: 1 year, both unopened and open.

Ground, canned coffee, unopened: 2 years. Opened: 2 weeks, if refrigerated.

Instant coffee in jars or cans, unopened: 12 months. Opened: 3 months.

Pudding mixes, unopened: 1 year. Opened: 4 months.
Jams, jellies, and preserves, unopened: 1 year. Opened: 6 months if refrigerated.
Peanut butter, unopened: 6–9 months. Opened: 2–3 months.

Useful Fruit Measures

1 teaspoon grated orange rind = ½ orange
3 tablespoons lemon juice = 1 lemon
1½ teaspoons grated lemon rind = 1 lemon
1 cup mashed banana = 3 medium bananas
6 tablespoons orange juice = 1 orange
1 cup orange juice = 3 medium oranges
1 cup chopped apple = 1 medium apple
4 cups sliced apples = 4 medium apples
4 cups sliced fresh peaches = 2 pounds or 8 medium peaches

Dairy

USEFUL SUBSTITUTIONS

1 teaspoon lemon juice = ½ teaspoon vinegar

1 tablespoon cornstarch = 2 tablespoons flour or 1 tablespoon arrowroot or 4 teaspoons quick-cooking tapioca

1 cup pre-sifted flour = 1 cup + 2 tablespoons sifted cake flour

1 cup sour milk/buttermilk = 1 cup milk + 1 tablespoon vinegar

⅔ cup honey = 1 cup sugar plus ⅓ cup water

1½ cups corn syrup = 1 cup sugar + ½ cup water

1 cup molasses = 1 cup honey + 1 tablespoon brown sugar

1 whole egg = 2 egg yolks + 1 tablespoon water

1 teaspoon oregano = 1 teaspoon marjoram

1 teaspoon allspice = ½ teaspoon cinnamon + ⅛ teaspoon cloves

Few drops of Tabasco = dash of cayenne or red pepper

½ cup plain nonfat yogurt = ½ cup mayonnaise

2 teaspoons baking soda + 1 cup buttermilk/sour milk = ½ teaspoon baking powder + 1 cup milk

1 ounce (25 grams) chocolate, unsweetened = 3–4 tablespoons cocoa + 1 tablespoon butter or margarine

1 teaspoon baking powder = ¼ teaspoon baking soda + ½ teaspoon cream of tartar

¾ cup cracker crumbs = 1 cup bread crumbs

1 cup heavy sour cream = ⅓ cup butter + ⅔ cup milk in any recipe calling for sour milk

1 cup whole milk = ½ cup evaporated milk + ½ cup water or 1 cup reconstituted nonfat dry milk + 1 tablespoon butter

2 ounces (50 grams) fresh yeast = 3 x ¼ oz (6 grams) packets of dry yeast

1 tablespoon minced onion, rehydrated = 1 small fresh onion

1 tablespoon prepared mustard = 1 teaspoon dry mustard

⅛ teaspoon garlic powder = 1 pressed clove of garlic

3 medium bananas = 1 cup mashed

3 cups dry corn flakes = 1 cup crushed

10 miniature marshmallows = 1 large marshmallow

1 cup fruit juice, for cooking = 1 cup brewed spicy herb tea

White wine = equal amount of apple juice or cider

½ cup balsamic vinegar = ½ cup red wine vinegar
  (slight flavor difference)

1 tablespoon tapioca = 1½ tablespoons flour

1 tablespoon brandy = ¼ teaspoon brandy extract plus
  1 tablespoon water

1 cup chili sauce = 1 cup tomato sauce + ¼ cup honey or
  sugar + 2 tablespoons vinegar (for use in cooked mixtures)

1 teaspoon mustard, dry = 1 tablespoon prepared mustard

1 teaspoon mustard, prepared = ¼ teaspoon dried mustard
  plus ¾ teaspoon vinegar

1 cup tomato juice = ½ cup tomato sauce + ½ cup water

2 cups tomato sauce = ¾ cup tomato paste + 1 cup water

CHEESE

Brie cheese has an edible white crust with a creamy yellow interior. It has a mild to pungent flavor. The rind is easy to trim from refrigerated brie or bring the cheese to room temperature, cut, and scoop out the soft center with a spoon.

· · · ·

Hard, underripe brie will probably not ripen. Purchase brie rounds that are no more than 1 inch (2.5 centimeters) thick, with a sweet odor. It should appear slightly bulging within the rind. The exterior should be firm, while the center should be springy but not watery. Thicker rounds will be overripe on the edges and underripe in the center.

. . . .

Underripe brie will feel hard when gently pressed with the finger, while overripe brie will feel too soft to the touch, have a brownish, gummy rind, and smell like ammonia.

. . . .

Ripe brie should be refrigerated and consumed within a few days. Ripe, uncut brie may be frozen up to six months. Brie should be brought to room temperature before eating.

. . . .

Camembert may be substituted for brie in equal measures. It has a stronger aroma and flavor than the brie.

. . . .

Camembert cheese has a grey-white edible crust and a creamy, soft interior. It has a mild to pungent flavor.

. . . .

Gouda cheese is a creamy yellow, often sold with a red wax coating. It has a mild, nutlike flavor.

. . . .

Gorgonzola cheese has a light tan surface, with a light yellow interior marbled with blue-green. It has a piquant, spicy flavor similar to Bleu Cheese.

. . . .

Roquefort cheese is white, marbled with blue-green, and sometimes crumbly. It has a sharp, spicy, piquant flavor. When buying Bleu or Roquefort cheese, avoid any with a brown color near the blue or green veins.

. . . .

Mozzarella should be moist, not dry or cracked. Store fresh mozzarella in the refrigerator in its own container. Refresh daily by pouring off some of the old water and adding a little fresh water, preferably bottled. Use fresh mozzarella balls within 1–2 days of opening and before the expiration date on the package. Do not use fresh mozzarella if it smells sour or has yellowed or dried out.

. . . .

Halloumi is not the most palatable cheese to nibble, but one that cooks very well and absorbs other flavors. It is good fried and served with a sauce or used in kebabs for vegetarian fare.

. . . .

Feta cheese is best preserved in a solution of half skim milk and half water that has been boiled and cooled. All cheeses should be served at room temperature.

. . . .

Parmesan cheese is a robust-flavored Italian cheese made with skim or part skim milk. It is often used grated, so not much is needed. Use in pasta dishes and salads.

. . . .

Store Parmesan cheese in an airtight container in the freezer; as it never freezes solid, it can be grated easily.

. . . .

Aged cheeses are low in moisture and can be frozen without much change in flavor or consistency. If it warms too fast, it becomes gritty. To thaw properly, take cheese from freezer, remove from wrapping, rewrap tightly, and thaw in refrigerator for 12–24 hours.

. . . .

Cheese must be kept refrigerated, but most cheese tastes better served at room temperature. Remove from the refrigerator 30–60 minutes before serving and keep covered. Exceptions include cream cheese and cottage cheese

. . . .

Spray cheese grater with oil for easy cleanup. Or try grating a raw potato after the cheese.

. . . .

A dull knife is more successful when cutting cheese than a sharp one. Crumbly cheese cuts easily with a warm knife.

. . . .

Shred cheese when it is cold. When it softens it is harder to shred. With soft texture cheese, use a grater with large holes or finely chop it.

. . . . .

Soak hard cheese in buttermilk to restore the moisture and soften it. Rejuvenate cheese that has started to dry out by sprinkling it with sugar.

. . . . .

Add beer to a cheese dish to intensify the flavor. Mustard and salt also bring out the flavor.

. . . . .

Cheese melts and blends better if shredded or cut into small pieces. Lower-fat cheeses do not melt well. Melt cheese on a low heat so the oils do not separate and the cheese become tough.

. . . . .

Grate leftover pieces of hard cheese and store in a plastic box or polyethylene bag in the refrigerator or freezer. Use for sauces, au gratin dishes, or in sandwiches.

"The cream of today is the cheese of tomorrow." —Unknown

Use a potato peeler to slice cheese into strips for salads and garnishes.

. . . . .

Roquefort or blue cheese will crumble perfectly for salads if kept in the freezer.

. . . . .

When using a block of cheese, slice the cheese on the flat with a potato peeler to get uniform cheese slices. Use a potato slicer on the corners of a block of cheese for quick shredded cheese.

. . . . .

Sprinkle nuts and cheese on top of food rather than mixing them throughout the dish.

. . . . .

When grilling or baking cheese-topped dishes, watch closely as the cheese may melt quickly and become overcooked.

. . . . .

Cheese microwaves well but use lower power settings.

. . . . .

To prevent losing the top layer of food when using aluminum foil to cover a dish with a cheese topping, spray the foil with cooking spray before covering the dish.

. . . . .

Top a casserole with cheese 5 minutes before end of cooking time. Use the broiler to achieve a golden top. This allows the cheese to remain soft and chewy, not hard and dry.

. . . .

To stop grated cheese from clumping together when freezing, put 1 teaspoon baking soda in the container of grated cheese and shake well before freezing.

. . . .

Put sugar cubes in cheese containers to keep the cheese free of mold.

. . . .

Cheese will not harden if the exposed edges are covered with butter before storing. Or wrap in fresh cabbage leaves. Renew leaves when withered. Wrap semisoft to hard cheese in foil.

. . . .

To stop cheese from going moldy, wrap it in cheesecloth wetted with white vinegar or salt water and keep in the refrigerator in a sealed container. Remoisten with vinegar as needed.

. . . .

Use a knife dipped in vinegar to slice mold off cheese. Dip after each slice to kill mold and prevent its reoccurrence.

. . . .

Soft cheeses to be sliced or used for processing should be placed in freezer 10–15 minutes before use.

. . . .

To make a flavored cream cheese, soften 8 ounces (225 grams) cream cheese and fold in 1 tablespoon each finely chopped onions and chives. Blend well. Refrigerate in an airtight container for up to 2 weeks.

. . . .

As a substitute for mascarpone cheese, beat 225 grams cream cheese until soft, add 3 ounces (75 grams) icing sugar, and beat until mixture is well combined. Add ½ pint (300 milliliters) cream and beat again until thick and creamy. Use in tiramisu recipes.

. . . .

Yogurt cheese has the same consistency as cream cheese but is lower in fat. Use as a spread or in cheesecake recipes. To make yogurt cheese, pour 1 pint (600 milliliters) yogurt into a large, fine-meshed strainer or colander lined with a double thickness of cheesecloth or a coffee filter. Place a bowl under the strainer to catch the liquid (whey) that drains from the yogurt. Cover the remaining yogurt and refrigerate for 8–24 hours (texture will vary depending on how long it drains). Save the calcium-rich whey to use in soups and gravies. Makes 1 cup of yogurt cheese.

. . . .

To speed-soften cream cheese for recipes, use a microwave oven. For 8 ounces (225 grams) cream cheese, microwave unwrapped at high for 30 seconds, or for 4 ounces (100 grams), microwave for 15 seconds. Leave for 1 minute before using.

. . . .

Always store cottage cheese and sour cream upside down in the refrigerator and they will last longer.

. . . .

"What butter and whiskey will not cure there's no cure for." —Unknown

Freezing adversely affects the texture of cottage cheese, sour cream, cooked eggs, yogurt, and mayonnaise.

· · · ·

Over-wrap blocks of butter in foil before freezing. Open freeze butter curls or pats before layering with greaseproof paper in a rigid container. Salted butter freezes for up to 3 months and unsalted for 6 months. If frozen butter is required urgently, grate it.

· · · ·

To prevent butter burning when frying with butter, add a little cooking oil or olive oil to the melting butter.

· · · ·

To make butter more spreadable when having to make a lot of sandwiches, beat 8 ounces (225 grams) butter, stir in 3 tablespoons hot water, and continue beating until combined.

· · · ·

For easy clarified butter, melt the butter in a saucepan. Slowly bring it to a gentle boil. Boil for 2 minutes. Remove from the heat and allow to cool. Cover and refrigerate overnight. Make a small hole near the edge. Carefully tilt the pan. The milk solids should easily drain off from the bottom, leaving the clarified butter. Reheat when required.

· · · ·

Use prune purée in place of butter in brownies, cakes, biscuits, and muffins. Exchange half the amount of prune purée, in place of the butter called for in the recipe. Process 8 ounces (225 grams) pitted prunes with 6 tablespoons (90 milliliters) hot water in a food processor until smooth. Prunes contain vitamin A, iron, potassium, and fiber.

CREAM, MILK & YOGURT

Evaporated milk can be used instead of heavy cream for whipping. Pour a can of evaporated milk into a bowl and chill in the freezer until ice crystals form, add 1 teaspoon lemon juice, and whip it until it is stiff.

. . . .

Do not freeze sour cream as it will separate on thawing. Cream must have a minimum fat content of 35 percent to freeze successfully.

. . . .

Whipped cream with 40 percent or more butterfat can be piped into rosettes and frozen before packing into a rigid container to store. Use within 2 months.

. . . .

Use powdered sugar to sweeten whipped cream; it not only dissolves quickly, but the cornstarch in it also helps stabilize the whipped cream.

. . . .

Keep in mind that cream will double in volume when it is whipped, so use a bowl that is big enough. Decrease splattering by gradually increasing the speed of the mixer from low to high. Drape a kitchen towel over the bowl of an electric standing mixer.

· · · · ·

Keep cream in the refrigerator until ready to whip. Chill the bowl and beaters in freezer for a few minutes. Whip only ½ pint (300 milliliters) at a time. Use a bowl just wide enough for the beaters. Whip just until soft peaks form. Over-beating can cause the cream to separate.

· · · · ·

Medium peaks retain marks of the whip and will hold a soft peak that droops over slightly. Stiff peaks will form distinct mounds that hold their shape. Over-beaten cream first develops a granular appearance. Eventually lumps will form and, if whipping continues, the cream will turn to butter.

· · · · ·

If whipping cream is accidentally over beaten and begins to turn buttery, gently stir in additional cream, 1 tablespoon at a time. Do not beat the cream again.

· · · · ·

To get more volume from whipped cream, do not add sugar or flavorings like vanilla until the cream has been whipped to soft peaks.

· · · · ·

A few drops of lemon juice or a pinch of salt added to whipping cream helps it whip faster and better. Salt added to the cream before whipping strengthens the fat cells and makes them more elastic. This helps the cream stiffen much more quickly.

· · · ·

To stabilize whipped cream, sprinkle ½ teaspoon unflavored gelatin in 1 tablespoon cold water and stir over low heat to dissolve. Leave to cool. Add to 1 cup heavy cream in a chilled bowl and whip until stiff. To keep cream for a longer period, add 1 teaspoon brandy to it.

· · · ·

To make a low-fat substitute for whipped cream, whip together ¼ cup (125 milliliters) cold water, 1 tablespoon lemon juice, ¾ cup (175 milliliters) skim milk powder, and a dash of salt for 8 minutes or until the mixture stands in stiff peaks. Gradually beat in 2 ounces (50 grams) sugar and ¼ teaspoon vanilla. Chill. Makes 1¾ pint (1 liter).

· · · ·

For whipped cream without a mixer, put cream in a chilled glass jar with a tight-fitting lid. Shake briskly for 5 minutes.

If a recipe calls for 1 cup sour cream, you can substitute with 1 cup cottage cheese blended until smooth with 1 tablespoon lemon juice and ⅓ cup buttermilk or ½ cup yogurt.

. . . .

Use sour cream instead of butter for frying. Heat it slowly to melt it, then cook with low heat.

. . . .

When heating milk, rinse the pan in cold water before pouring in the milk and it will not stick to the pan. Or heat the pan by boiling a little water in it, then discard before adding the milk. Or sprinkle bottom of the pan with granulated sugar.

. . . .

Leave a spoon in the pan in which milk is being boiled at low heat so that it does not burn at the bottom.

. . . .

While boiling milk, if there is any chance of the milk splitting, add a pinch of baking soda.

. . . .

To keep milk from scorching, add a pinch of sugar while cooking and do not stir.

. . . .

To remove the burnt taste from scorched milk, place the hot pan in cold water and add a dash of salt.

. . . .

Before freezing milk, pour off a little from the top to allow room for expansion as it freezes. Two days before milk is required, remove it from freezer and defrost in refrigerator. You can freeze extra milk in an ice cube tray and put into bags when frozen.

. . . .

Place a wooden spoon in a saucepan of milk just before it comes to a boil and the milk will not boil over.

. . . .

If milk begins to boil over, quickly sprinkle a little cold water over it and the overflow will subside.

. . . .

Adding a pinch of salt to milk will keep it fresh longer.

. . . .

To avoid a skin forming on boiled milk, add 1 teaspoon water to it.

. . . .

Stop milk dripping from a milk jug by smearing the lip with a little butter.

. . . .

Buttermilk is low fat or skim milk to which a bacterial culture has been added. Milk soured with lemon juice or vinegar can be substituted for buttermilk. Or use ½ cup milk plus ¾ cup plain yogurt for each cup of buttermilk.

. . . .

For homemade sweetened condensed milk, in a blender combine 2 cups powdered milk, ½ cup hot (not boiling) water, 1 cup granulated sugar, and 3 tablespoons butter. Blend smooth to dissolve sugar. Store covered in refrigerator.

. . . . .

Yogurt can be used in place of sour cream. Do not boil because it tends to separate.

. . . . .

To make yogurt, combine 2 pints (1.2 liters) whole milk with 2 tablespoons dried milk and heat to 180°F. Remove from the heat and allow to cool to 110°F. Add 3 tablespoons plain yogurt and stir well. Pour into sterilized jars or a thermos flask. Leave in a warm place to incubate for 4–12 hours. Do not stir. To use, refrigerate until cool and add sugar, honey, or chopped fruit as desired. In an airtight container, yogurt will last for about 8 days in the refrigerator.

. . . . .

If homemade yogurt does not thicken this may be due to:
· The milk being too hot or too cold when starter was added.
· Not enough starter added.
· The incubating temperature was too low or too high.
· You need to incubate longer; though it will be tart, it will eventually set.
· Yogurt mixture was moved or disturbed during incubation.
· Starter too old or inactive due to no live active culture.

. . . . .

If yogurt becomes grainy during cooking, stabilize by mixing 5 milliliters cornstarch with a little water and add to the dish. Continue cooking.

. . . .

Store-bought yogurts can be frozen unopened for 6 weeks. To defrost, thaw at room temperature for 3 hours, or place yogurt in the refrigerator overnight. Fruit yogurt freezes for 3 months and plain for 2 months. Do not freeze Greek-style yogurt as it separates on thawing.

. . . .

Crème fraîche is a rich, thick cream with a mild, tangy flavor that is similar to sour cream but not as sour. It is used like whipping cream in sauces, soups, or desserts. It can be boiled without curdling and whipped to soft peaks.

. . . .

For homemade crème fraîche, combine 1 cup whipping cream with 2 tablespoons fresh cultured buttermilk in a saucepan. Heat the mixture to 110°F, pour into a glass container, and leave at room temperature overnight, loosely covered, until it is very thick and has a mild sour flavor. Cover tightly and refrigerate for up to a week in an airtight container.

Baking Bonanza

PREPARING TO BAKE

Always read the recipe over at least once before starting. Check your supply of ingredients and note any unusual ingredients, equipment required, and cooking instructions.

. . . .

Use baking pans of good quality; thin, flimsy sheets do not diffuse heat well or evenly and can result in the base of the baking being scorched. A dark metal pan or baking sheet will bake faster than a shiny metal pan.

. . . .

Have good fresh ingredients. Spices lose their flavor over time so check the date on jars. Use the best affordable ingredients. Unless stated otherwise, all ingredients should be at room temperature.

. . . .

Clear the work area before commencing and assemble all the ingredients. Rinse bowls and utensils as you go.

. . . .

Use cold water to remove flour and hot water to wipe sugar off countertops.

. . . .

Always place ingredients on the LEFT before using them, and to the far RIGHT after use. This way if interrupted while cooking it is easy to see what has already been added.

. . . .

Do not grease a baking pan with margarine or butter as they contain salt and can cause hot foods to stick. Use oil or solid shortening.

. . . .

Line baking pans with wax or parchment paper to prevent sticking.

. . . .

Leave a 2-inch (5-centimeter) space between the oven walls and the baking sheet for good circulation.

. . . .

Cooking and baking times specified in most recipes are merely guidelines. Since oven temperatures can vary from oven to oven, it is best to check the dish a few minutes before recommended.

. . . .

Do not open the oven more than necessary. It wastes energy, increases cooking time, and can lower the temperature by 25°F.

. . . .

Preheat an oven for 15 minutes before baking foods such as bread, pastry, and cakes. Foods requiring 1 hour or more of baking can be started in a cold oven, but this must be factored into the recipe's baking time. Most ovens have hot spots. To ensure even baking, rotate baking dishes and pans from top to bottom and from front to back.

BAKING

Glass or ceramic dishes retain heat better than metal so the oven cooking temperature can be reduced by 25°F.

. . . .

To test oven temperatures without a thermometer, spread a small amount of flour ¼ inch (50 millimeters) thick on the bottom of an inverted metal pan and place in oven. If it turns a delicate brown in 5 minutes the oven is slow while golden brown is moderate. If it turns a golden brown in 3 minutes the oven is hot while if it is dark golden brown it is very hot.

. . . . .

When taking the cooked pan of cookies out of the oven, close the door and wait a few minutes for the temperature to stabilize before putting in a new pan.

. . . . .

Baking cakes and other treats is not always cheaper from scratch, especially if ingredients have to be purchased that are not always kept on hand.

. . . . .

To measure flour, stir it in the bag or canister to lighten it. Gently spoon flour into a dry measuring cup or measuring spoons. Level it off with the straight side of a knife.

. . . . .

When a recipe calls for 1 cup sifted flour it means it should be sifted first. When it calls for 1 cup flour sifted, it means it should be measured before sifting it.

. . . . .

When a recipe requires cake flour, but only all-purpose flour is available, sift the all-purpose flour about 5 times. Or put 2 teaspoons cornstarch in a measuring cup, fill the remainder of the cup with flour, and sift well to blend.

. . . . .

When out of self-rising flour, add 2½ level teaspoons baking powder and ½ teaspoon salt to 8 ounces (225 grams) plain flour when baking cakes, or for scones add 3 level teaspoons baking powder. If baking powder is not available, use ½ level teaspoon baking soda and 1 level teaspoon cream of tartar, sifted together 2–3 times.

· · · ·

A little salt added to flour before adding liquid will keep it from lumping.

· · · ·

In hot weather, keep pests out of flour by putting a bay leaf or a wrapped stick of spearmint gum in the container and seal or store flour in the freezer.

· · · ·

If butter is not softened ahead of time, cut the block into thin pats and place them on a room temperature plate. Leave in a warm area for 10 minutes until the butter yields to gentle finger pressure.

When using butter in place of vegetable shortening, the amount of butter should be ¼ more than the amount of shortening.

. . . .

When adding flour and liquids alternately, ensure the flour is the first and last ingredient added.

. . . .

It is best to cream butter by itself before adding the sugar.

. . . .

It will take 8–10 minutes to properly cream butter and sugar using the slow or medium speed of a hand-held electric mixer. Do not use high speed to cream these ingredients.

. . . .

Measure liquids at eye level. Place the cup on a flat surface and look at the same level as the cup in order to make sure of having the correct amount.

. . . .

When melted chocolate is added to a batter, add it after creaming the fat and sugar and before any eggs or liquid.

. . . .

When working with dough, do not flour your hands; coat them with olive oil to prevent sticking.

. . . .

Active dry yeast is compressed yeast from which the moisture has been removed. It needs to be reactivated with water before use and is recommended for traditional baking and not for use in bread-making machines. Instant yeast is a combination of dried yeast with the bread improver Vitamin C (ascorbic acid). It can be added straight to the dough mixture.

· · · · ·

Yeast will last longer than the specified date printed on the packet if kept in the refrigerator or up to a year in the freezer. Place in a tightly sealed plastic container and label. Bring to room temperature before using.

· · · · ·

Dissolve 1 teaspoon granulated sugar into ½ cup warm water. Sprinkle 1 packet of yeast slowly over the surface of the water. Stir the yeast mixture and leave for 10 minutes. If the yeast has multiplied to the 1 cup mark and has a rounded crown, the yeast is still active and fresh and you may use it. Remember to deduct ½ cup of liquid from the total amount of liquid used in the recipe.

· · · · ·

Expired packages of yeast can usually be brought back long after the package date by "proofing" the yeast. Mix ¼ cup rewarmed water used for boiling potatoes, 1 teaspoon sugar, and 1 envelope of yeast. Leave in a warm place. If it bubbles and doubles in bulk in 6–10 minutes, use it. Otherwise, discard.

BREAD-MAKING

Soft, pure water is best suited for bread-making purposes. Hard water can neutralize the fermentation produced by the yeast.

. . . . .

Yeast breads are moister when made with potato water than with other liquids. It keeps the bread fresh for longer and gives it a slightly greater volume but coarser texture.

. . . . .

If yeast was not added to dough, do not start over. Dissolve the required yeast in sugar and water as usual and, when it is ready, knead it into the mixture and let the dough rise.

. . . . .

Kneading is a crucial step in gluten development for breads, basically making them elastic and springy.

. . . . .

For standard yeast bread, gather well-blended dough on countertop and keep extra flour handy. With the heel of your hand, push the dough into the countertop away from you and fold it back over itself toward you, adding a bit more flour only as needed. Turn 90 degrees and repeat. Continue doing this until the dough is smooth and elastic, usually 10–15 minutes.

. . . . .

Try kneading bread dough in a plastic bag. Place the dough in a large bag to rise. Leave it there when working it down and kneading it. Or knead in a large bowl.

. . . . .

When kneading, keep a couple of small plastic bags within reach. Then if the telephone rings or someone is at the door, slip your hands into the bags.

. . . .

To test if dough is ready for proving, poke the dough with a finger and it should spring back. Also, try gently stretching the dough between your hands, it should not tear. When finished kneading cover dough and let rise once or twice.

. . . .

Use nonstick cooking spray to oil the inside of the bowl used to raise yeast dough; also spray the top of the dough.

. . . .

Place the kneaded dough in the oiled bowl to rise. Cover it loosely with plastic wrap. Place a clean, damp kitchen towel in the microwave for 30–50 seconds and then use it to cover the plastic wrap and down the sides of the bowl. The heat and moisture from the towel help make the dough rise more quickly. The towel can be reheated a second time.

. . . .

To get yeast dough to rise faster, turn the dishwasher dial to "dry" for a minute to warm the inside, then put the dough inside the dishwasher.

. . . .

Make a "proofing box" using a large picnic cooler. Pour 2 pints (1.2 liters) of boiling water into the bottom. Set a rack in the cooler so it sits above the water level. Set the bowl with the bread dough in it on the rack and close the lid.

. . . .

Give slow dough a boost with the warmth of an electric heating pad. Put the bread pans on the warm pad, covering them with waxed paper and a clean tea towel. Or rest them on a cloth-covered hot water bottle. Pans of dough can be put into a cold oven with a pot of boiling water; the heat and moisture will encourage them to rise. The most convenient place for yeast bread to rise is the inside of a switched-off oven with the light on.

. . . .

To test if dough has doubled in size, stick the fingertips about ½ inch (50 millimeters) into the dough. If the impressions stay, the dough has doubled.

. . . .

If interrupted when bread-making, set the dough in the refrigerator. A long, cool rise develops texture and flavor.

When planning on making yeast dough to freeze for later use, add a little extra yeast to the recipe.

. . . .

Clean a credit card and use it to scrape dough from the bottom of a bowl or off a cutting board.

. . . .

When yeast dough has been kneaded to develop elasticity, it will fight the rolling pin when trying to roll it out. Allow it to relax for 10–15 minutes and it will be stretchy again.

. . . .

For a soft, well-browned but not shiny crust, before baking brush the loaf with 1 tablespoon melted butter. For a slightly brown and crisper crust, after 20 minutes of baking, brush the bread with an egg beaten in 1 tablespoon milk.

. . . .

Brushing bread with salty water before baking gives it a lovely crunchy topping.

. . . .

Too much salt, even in slight quantities, interferes with the proper aeration of the dough resulting in making the loaf smaller and the crust losing its golden brown color and becoming a dull grey. Use 1 tablespoon sugar to each 1 pound (450 grams) bread. Too much sugar in bread gives toughness to both crumb and crust.

. . . .

To glaze the tops of rolls, brush with a mixture of 1 tablespoon sugar and ¼ cup milk before baking.

. . . . .

Roll bread dough flat and spread with crushed garlic and herbs. Roll up and bake as directed.

. . . . .

Try using both yeast and baking powder in pizza dough. Use high gluten flour. Use 1 ounce (25 grams) dough portion for every 1 inch (2.5 centimeters) pizza diameter. Store individual raw dough portions dusted with flour in self-sealing plastic bags in refrigerator up to a week or in freezer up to a month. Bake on a pizza stone for crisper crust.

. . . . .

Make pizza dough in double batches and freeze half. Roll out the extra dough, fit it into a pizza pan, and freeze it flat.

. . . . .

To cool a loaf of yeast bread, remove loaves from pans immediately and place on wire racks. To have a softer crust, brush the loaf with shortening and cover with a towel for a few minutes.

. . . . .

Determine the doneness of bread by tapping the crust. The loaf will have a hollow sound when done.

. . . . .

Flat loaves can be caused by too soft dough.

. . . . .

Porous bread can be due to over-rising or cooking at too low a temperature.

. . . .

A dark crust with blisters under is due to under-rising.

. . . .

Un-risen bread can be due to over-kneading or using old yeast.

. . . .

Bread that is streaked can be due to not kneading enough.

. . . .

Unevenly baked bread can be due to using old, dark pans or too much dough in pans or crowding the oven shelf or cooking at too high a temperature.

. . . .

A strong yeasty aroma means too much yeast was added. Heavy bread can be a result of adding too much flour or not enough liquid.

. . . .

If bread is too brown, too much sugar was added.

. . . .

Badly risen bread may be caused by too much sugar or fat added to the recipe.

. . . .

Too much baking powder or baking soda added to a bread batter can give the bread a crumbly, dry texture and a bitter aftertaste. It can also make the loaf over-rise and then fall on removal from the oven.

. . . .

Fresh bread that is too difficult to slice should be placed in the freezer for 10–15 minutes and it will slice easily.

. . . .

To cut fresh bread or cake without crumbling, use a thin bladed knife heated in hot water, then dried.

. . . .

The easiest way to cut bread cubes is to first freeze the bread, then trim and cube a stack of frozen slices.

. . . .

Mix batches of the dry ingredients of a favorite recipe and store them in individual plastic bags, clearly labeled, in the refrigerator. The mix will be ready when required.

. . . .

To butter many slices of bread quickly and evenly, heat the butter until soft, then "paint" it on with a flat pastry brush.

. . . .

To warm bread before serving, place the bread in a paper bag, seal it, and moisten a portion of the outside of the bag. Place it in a preheated oven at 350°F/180°C/Gas 4 for 5–6 minutes. Bread will be warmed and ready to serve.

. . . .

Place aluminum foil under the napkin in a roll basket and the rolls will stay hot longer.

. . . .

To revive day-old tortillas, place tortillas on a large piece of waxed paper, fold the open edges to make a packet, and microwave on high for 15–25 seconds.

. . . .

To steam a tortilla, wet a paper towel, squeeze out the excess water, roll up the tortilla in the towel. Heat for 25 seconds in the microwave on high power, then unroll the towel.

. . . .

Dry or crisp older bread for croutons in the microwave.

. . . .

To make croutons, brush slices of bread with melted butter and season to taste. Cut into cubes and place in a single layer on a baking sheet. Bake at 250°F/120°C/Gas ½ for 10 minutes, stir, and bake for a further 10 minutes. Or cook in ungreased heavy skillet over medium heat 4–7 minutes, stirring frequently, until golden brown.

. . . .

To make breadcrumbs, dry out stale bread in a microwave until crisp, place in a strong sealed bag, and crush with a rolling pin. For seasoned breadcrumbs, toast old bread, leave to harden, break into small pieces, and place in a blender. Add black pepper, garlic salt, oregano, and onion salt, and blend till crumbed. Put in freezer bag and freeze for up to 6 months.

. . . .

Place stale and hardened bread, bagels, and rolls in a plastic bag and store in the freezer. When breadcrumbs are required, take out a piece of the bread and rub it across a cheese grater.

. . . . .

Keep bread fresh longer by placing a rib of celery in the bread bag. Put bread in the refrigerator and it will keep fresh well past the use by date.

. . . . .

Keep picnic sandwiches from becoming soggy by spreading the mayonnaise or mustard between the slices of meat instead of on the bread.

. . . . .

To make melba toast, cut stale bread into quarters and bake in a low oven until crisp. Or toast thick cut slices of bread and cut through each slice with a sharp knife. Cut into quarters and place the untoasted side under the grill until crispy.

. . . . .

Dip slices of stale bread in sweetened condensed milk and then roll in flaked coconut. Put them on a baking sheet in a hot oven and cook just until the coconut turns brown and the bread is hot.

. . . . .

Honey can be used instead of sugar in a bread or cake recipe. Since honey is sweeter than sugar, use a 4–5 ratio. For 5 tablespoons sugar, use 4 tablespoons honey. Decrease any water added to the recipe by 2 teaspoons per cup of honey used and add a pinch of baking soda to balance out the pH of the mixture and allow it to rise properly.

. . . . .

When making griddle cakes, grease the pan for the first cake. After that, rub a piece of raw potato over the hot griddle instead of more grease. The cakes brown well and the pan does not smoke.

．．．．

When making fruit scones, add 1 tablespoon marmalade to the mixture to keep them moist.

．．．．

Butter and margarine are interchangeable if both are listed in the ingredient list. Do not use low fat spreads or soft or tub margarine unless recipe specifically calls for these ingredients. They act differently in baking or cooking and may cause unsatisfactory results.

．．．．

For quick and easy garlic breadsticks, split a hot dog bun down the middle and cut each half lengthways. Butter each strip; sprinkle with garlic salt or garlic powder. Place on a cookie sheet and bake or grill until toasted.

"The smell of good bread baking, like the sound of lightly flowing water, is indescribable in its evocation of innocence and delight." —M. F. K. Fisher

To thaw frozen bread and rolls, place in a brown paper bag and put into a preheated oven at 325°F/160°C/Gas 3 for 5 minutes to thaw completely.

. . . .

Rub slices of burnt toast against one another rather than scraping them. It leaves the toast in better condition.

. . . .

Sprinkling lemon juice over bread before frying prevents greasiness and adds flavor.

PANCAKES

Use a meat baster to squeeze pancake batter onto the hot griddle for perfectly shaped pancakes.

. . . .

Prevent batter from sticking to a mixer's beaters by spraying them with nonstick cooking oil before submerging them.

. . . .

To prevent pancakes or waffles from sticking to the griddle, rub down with salt.

. . . .

For the very lightest pancakes, replace liquid with club soda. Use all the batter as it will go flat if stored.

. . . .

Substitute water with beer when making batter. Beer batter will fry crisper and lighter if allowed to stand awhile before mixing. This gives the flour granules time to soften and absorb the liquid.

. . . . .

Add 2 teaspoons vinegar to pancake dough when making a large batch of pancakes for freezing. When the pancakes are defrosted and heated in the microwave they taste like fresh baked and not tough.

. . . . .

To jazz up pancakes, French toast, or waffles, add a dash or two of cinnamon and/or vanilla to the batter.

. . . . .

Pancake batter or biscuit dough slides right off a pouring spoon dipped in milk.

. . . . .

Do not over-mix pancake batter; stir the batter until moistened. Flip the pancakes once. When they begin to bubble, it is time to turn them.

. . . . .

When cooking pancakes, the griddle is ready when a drop of water dances on the heated surface and then quickly evaporates.

. . . . .

To make extra-light, airy pancakes, separate the eggs and mix the yolks into the batter first. Beat the whites until stiff and fold in at the end.

. . . . .

Add some chopped banana to a batch of pancakes
for a very tasty treat.

. . . .

For extra-light pancakes, try substituting apple cider for the milk
called for in the recipe.

. . . .

Cool leftover pancakes, then place them in a freezer-proof
container separated by waxed-paper squares. Seal and freeze for
up to 3 months.

. . . .

For pancake syrup, mix 1 cup brown sugar and ¾ cup water in a
saucepan, bring to the boil, and simmer for 15 minutes. Do not
reboil or overcook. Add 1 teaspoon maple flavoring.

Pastry & Pies

The secret to good pastry making is to ensure that the
ingredients are measured exactly. Sieve the flour at least three
times. This is not to remove any lumps but to evenly distribute
the gluten content. Add a little lemon juice to encourage the
gluten strands to relax and shorten.

. . . .

Handle the pastry as lightly as possible—when rubbing in the fat
use fingertips only and lift them into the air to allow air to get
into the pastry and make it lighter, more delicate.

. . . .

Combine the dry ingredients by adding the cold liquid slowly and avoid using too much or the pastry will be hard and tough. For best results, pie dough should be worked very lightly after the water has been added.

. . . . .

Each and every time the pastry is handled allow it to rest for at least 30 minutes in the refrigerator. This allows the gluten strands to relax again, as each time it is handled they are stretched out.

. . . . .

Roll pastry between two sheets of plastic wrap, parchment, or waxed paper; no extra flour will be required and it is easier to lift the pastry without breaking it. Dampen the countertop to prevent the plastic from moving.

. . . . .

Instead of flouring the rolling pin, chill the rolling pin in the freezer and the dough will not stick.

. . . . .

If you tend to over-stretch pastry, when lining the tin, leave some surplus around the edge when trimming the pastry. Leave in a cool place for 30 minutes before using.

. . . . .

For extremely flaky pie pastry, measure the flour and fat into the bowl and chill at least an hour before mixing.

. . . . .

*"You will never 'find' time for anything.
If you want time, you must make it."* —Charles Buxton

Use vegetable shortening for pie dough to give it a flaky crust.
Use half as much fat as flour.

· · · ·

A food processor makes good shortcrust pastry but do not over-process. Use short bursts of power to blend butter into flour. Use only enough water to make ingredients cling together; too much water causes shrinkage.

· · · ·

To make a lighter pastry, use soda water and a few drops of lemon juice. For flakier piecrusts, add 1 teaspoon vinegar to the cold water when preparing the dough.

· · · ·

Pastry being served cold will be crisper if whole milk or light cream is used instead of water to mix the ingredients.

· · · ·

Pastry made with cold water is flaky. Pastry made with hot water is crumbly.

· · · ·

Always roll backward and forward as side-to-side rolling makes the pastry rise unevenly. Successful pastry needs to be kept cool throughout the making process and baked in a hot oven.

· · · ·

To easily roll out pastry, place half the dough on a piece of waxed paper and cover with a second piece. Roll out the pastry between the paper layers, using a light touch. Remove the top piece of waxed paper and flip the pastry into the pan with the bottom sheet. Peel off the waxed paper. Repeat the process for the top crust.

. . . . .

Use a pastry scraper to clean off the counter after rolling out pastry or kneading bread. A piece of dry bread crust will gather up the traces of flour.

. . . . .

To get rolled pastry off the board and into the pie pan, fold it lightly in half, then in half again. Unfold it in the pie tin.

. . . . .

Roll leftover pie dough out ¼ inch (50 millimeters) thick. Place on a baking sheet, sprinkle with cinnamon and sugar mixture, then bake in 375°F/190°C/Gas 5 oven until lightly browned.

. . . . .

When working with filo (phyllo) pastry dough, keep the box refrigerated until ready to use it. If frozen, thaw it in the refrigerator overnight. Have all other ingredients and equipment ready before removing pastry from the box. Do not work in direct sunlight.

Unroll filo pastry onto a work surface and keep it covered with a slightly damp towel. Do not allow sheets to become too wet or they will stick together. Cover the leaves not being used to keep them from drying out.

. . . . .

Any remaining sheets should be chilled and used up as soon as possible; place back in the original packaging and also wrap in plastic wrap to keep out the air. It can be frozen but does not yield the best results once defrosted again. Only use filo pastry with ingredients that cook quickly.

. . . . .

A blind baked pastry shell means cooking the pastry shell without a filling. To avoid a soggy pastry base, roll the pastry no more than 5 millimeters thick and line the tin. Lightly pierce the base with a fork to stop air bubbles forming. Cover the pastry case with parchment and fill with baking beans (these can be the reusable synthetic type or any kind of dried beans). Allow to rest for at least 30 minutes in the refrigerator before placing in the preheated oven, 350°F/180°C/Gas 4 and baking for 20 minutes. Remove from oven, remove the baking beans and parchment, brush with a little egg wash, and return to the oven for another 5–10 minutes. This will seal the pastry and prevent it from absorbing any moisture from the filling used. Remove from the oven and allow to cool before using.

. . . . .

When pie recipes call for dotting the filling with butter, rub the cold butter over the coarse side of a cheese grater and sprinkle the grated butter over the top. This allows the butter to be more evenly distributed over the pie.

. . . . .

Save the drained unsweetened juice from defrosted or canned fruit and use the juice when cooking fruit for pies.

· · · · ·

Before freezing fruit for pies, store it in a sealed, airtight plastic bag and place the bag in a pie tin. The fruit will freeze in the shape of the tin so that when required to add it to the crust, it will fit perfectly without gaps.

· · · · ·

Never put hot or warm filling into a raw piecrust. Bake the shell for 5–10 minutes or until lightly browned.

· · · · ·

Prevent soggy crust when making a custard-style pie by carefully breaking one of the eggs for the pie filling into the unbaked pastry shell. Swirl it around so the egg white covers the entire surface and then pour the egg into the filling mixture.

· · · · ·

When baking a custard pie, heat the milk to the boiling point before mixing it with the eggs. This also helps to keep the bottom crust crisp.

For the perfect, smooth custard top, do not over-beat the eggs with milk or cream as it can create air bubbles.

. . . .

To fold whipped cream into custard, first stir a spoonful of the cream into the custard to lighten it, then turn that mixture into the whipped cream. Using a rubber spatula, cut straight down through the center of the mixture then turn the spatula toward you and lift up. Turn the bowl slightly and repeat. Continue the folding procedure, working quickly around the bowl until no streaks remain.

. . . .

Bake custard pies at a high temperature for the first 10 minutes to prevent a soggy crust, then lower temperature for the remainder of the baking time.

. . . .

For custard pies, cook the custard first in a well-greased pie pan, without the crust. Chill in pan. Then carefully remove and place into a cooled, prebaked piecrust of the same size.

. . . .

To prevent a soggy crust when making cream pies, spread a layer of finely ground nuts, equal parts of sugar and flour, unseasoned dry breadcrumbs, or fine cookie crumbs on the bottom crust before adding the filling. Use crumbs from ginger biscuits when making an apple pie.

. . . .

For streusel pies, mix together ⅓ cup peanut butter and ¾ cup powdered sugar. Spread on the bottom of a baked pie shell. Cover it with a favorite cream pie recipe.

. . . .

For a quick topping for a berry pie, whip together 1 container sour cream, ½ cup milk, and 1 packet instant pudding.

. . . .

When cooking tart fruits such as rhubarb, apricots, grapes, or red raspberries, add a generous amount of cinnamon. For grapes, add vanilla too, for a different flavor.

. . . .

Use a little red food coloring and 1–2 drops almond extract to cherry pies when using fresh or canned cherries. Add a little yellow food coloring and 1 teaspoon lemon juice to apricot and peach fruit pies. The lemon juice will enhance their flavor and keep a bright color.

. . . .

When making apple pies, put a layer of apples on the pastry base, then the sugar, cinnamon, and lemon juice, and then another layer of apples. Cover with the pastry top. This will ensure that the pies do not run over in the oven.

. . . .

Do not cut apples for pies into pieces too thin; larger chunks will hold together and have more apple flavor.

. . . .

Put a layer of lemon curd on the base of an apple tart or add raisins to the chopped apples to give a different flavor.

. . . .

When making mincemeat pies, remove the lid from the jar of mincemeat and place the jar in the microwave for a few seconds and it will be easier to spoon into the tart shells.

. . . .

To stop soft fruit tarts or mince pies from leaking juice during cooking, sprinkle cornstarch or 1 tablespoon quick-cooking tapioca over the filling before covering with pastry.

. . . .

When making cream pies, keep them firm for cutting by adding half a packet of unflavored gelatin.

. . . .

Do not over-cook pie fillings, especially those with cornstarch used as the thickener. The filling will break down and quickly become watery. Over-cooking fillings made with flour will make the filling thick.

. . . .

For a decorative top piecrust, use a thimble to cut holes and replace the cuttings back in their holes. The holes will get bigger as the pie bakes, making an interesting pattern.

. . . .

To keep the top crust attached to the lower crust of a pie, moisten the bottom edge with beaten egg yolk or milk before pressing the edges together. Fold the top crust over the lower crust before crimping to keep the juices in the pie while baking.

. . . . .

Glaze the top of double-crust fruit pies to make them look and taste special. Brush the unbaked top crust with milk, water, beaten egg, egg white, or melted butter; then sprinkle lightly with sugar.

. . . . .

For a shiny piecrust, brush on a little vinegar for the last few minutes of cooking time.

. . . . .

A piecrust edge will not burn if the center is cut out of a foil pie plate leaving a 1-inch (2.5-centimeter) rim and turned upside down over the pie as it bakes. Remove during the last 5 minutes of baking.

. . . . .

To thicken juices of fresh fruit fillings, use 1 tablespoon quick-cooking tapioca instead of the all-purpose flour the recipe calls for. Juices will be clear and it adds a great texture to the pie.

. . . . .

Put a layer of miniature marshmallows in the bottom of a pumpkin pie, then add the filling. The marshmallows will rise to the top and give a nice topping.

. . . . .

To prevent juice spills when baking pies, cut several 3-inch (7.5-centimeter) lengths of tubular macaroni and poke them into the piecrust before placing in the oven. Heated juices will rise up into the hollow macaroni instead of spilling over into the oven.

. . . .

Baking a pie on a pizza stone absorbs excess moisture and makes the bottom crust crisper.

. . . .

Fruit pies can be stored at room temperature for a short period of time. Cover and refrigerate any pies with fillings that contain eggs or dairy products.

. . . .

Brush frozen pies with melted butter before baking. The butter eliminates the dryness that freezing causes.

. . . .

Use a buttered knife to cut through a soft pie.

Eggs

Fresh eggs should not be washed until ready for use because they are protected with a soluble film that protects the porous shell against bacteria.

. . . .

"Love and eggs are best when they are fresh." —*Russian proverb*

While raw eggs may be kept refrigerated in their closed container for several weeks, cooked eggs in the shell will only keep up to 7 days refrigerated, and shelled, cooked eggs kept covered last only 5 days. Cooked eggs should never be kept at room temperature for more than 2 hours.

. . . .

Cook egg whites before use in all recipes for full safety in chilled desserts, frosting, or icing. Use a heavy saucepan, the top of a double boiler, or a metal bowl placed over water in a saucepan. Stir together the egg whites from the recipe, 2 tablespoons sugar per egg white, 1 teaspoon water per egg white, and ⅛ teaspoon cream of tartar for every 2 egg whites. Cook over low heat or simmering water, beating constantly with a portable mixer at low speed, until the whites reach 160°F. Pour into a large bowl. Beat on high speed until the whites stand in soft peaks. Proceed with the recipe. Note that you must use sugar to keep the whites from coagulating too rapidly. Test with a thermometer as there is no visual clue to doneness. If you use an unlined aluminum saucepan, eliminate the cream of tartar or the two will react and create an unattractive gray meringue.

. . . .

Traditional mousse recipes, using raw egg whites, are generally safe to eat because they incorporate whipping cream with 35% fat. The fat content in the whipping cream inhibits food poisoning from the raw egg whites in the same way that oil does with raw eggs in mayonnaise.

. . . .

When using raw egg in an unbaked recipe, coddle the egg: Put the whole egg on a spoon and dip it into boiling water for 40 seconds. Shock the egg in cold water to stop the cooking process.

. . . .

Make sure that any cooked part of a mousse recipe is well cooled before folding in whipped cream or beaten egg whites. Hot mixtures will deflate the foam very quickly.

. . . .

Always use the egg size that is called for in the recipe. If the size is not given, assume that it is large. Most eggs used in baking should be at room temperature.

. . . .

Break every egg by itself, in a saucer, before putting it into a pan in case there should be any bad ones that may spoil the others. Eggs are easiest to separate when cold.

CAKES

Before baking a cake, ensure the cake pan is the correct size. If a ring cake pan is required but none is available, place a handleless, ovenproof mug in the center of a round, deep casserole dish.

. . . .

If no removable base cake pan is available, fold a strip of tin foil and press into the tin with the ends hanging out. It will help when removing the cake from the pan.

. . . .

Bright shiny baking pans make more evenly baked cakes.

. . . .

Cake flour should be low in gluten content. A medium to high gluten flour will give a heavy-textured, non-risen cake.

. . . .

Flour should be sieved 2–3 times from a reasonable height from sieve to bowl.

. . . .

For best results in cake baking, let eggs, butter, and milk reach room temperature before mixing.

. . . .

When egg whites are to be folded into a mixture, they should be beaten to soft peaks only, as this softer consistency will allow them to be folded into a stiffer mixture without deflating and releasing the air that had been carefully beaten in.

. . . .

Fold beaten egg whites into a thicker mixture with a gentle over-and-under lifting motion.

. . . .

When blending butter and sugar, heating the mixture in the microwave can make it too runny. Rinse a bowl with hot water, then dry completely and add butter and sugar. The heat is enough to produce a good creamed mixture.

. . . .

When creaming butter and sugar together, beat the sugar gradually into softened butter to ensure it is absorbed, then beat on high speed until mixture is light and fluffy. A tablespoon of boiling water can be added to the mixture for a lighter cake texture.

. . . . .

To replace an egg when baking a cake, use 1 tablespoon vinegar or 10 milliliters of lemon juice and 25 milliliters of milk. Use for replacing 1 egg only or the flavor will be too strong.

. . . . .

Add 1 tablespoon (15 milliliters) peanut butter to the fruit cake mixture for a nutty taste.

. . . . .

Sift ¼ teaspoon dry mustard with each 8 ounces (225 grams) flour when baking rich fruitcakes for a mellow fruity flavor.

. . . . .

When making a fruitcake add 1 tablespoon ground almonds to the mixture and this will keep the cake moist for longer. Store in an airtight tin or in the refrigerator.

. . . . .

Darken the color and increase the flavor of a fruitcake by substituting strong black coffee for the milk required. In a boiled fruitcake use cold tea instead of water.

. . . . .

"Flattery is like cake—if it causes you to want more, you have had too much." —Unknown

To prevent nuts and fruits from sinking to the bottom of a cake during baking, warm them a short time in the oven and then toss in flour. Shake off excess flour before mixing into the batter.

. . . .

Dried fruit will chop much easier if it is placed in the freezer one hour before planning to start chopping.

. . . .

When making a rich fruitcake, keep some of the non-fruited mixture aside. After putting the fruited mixture into the cake tin, spread the non-fruited mixture over the top. This prevents having burnt bits of fruit on the surface and makes icing easier.

. . . .

If a cake recipe calls for lemon zest, grate the lemon using the finest grate on the grater.

. . . .

For a moist chocolate cake, add 1 tablespoon mayonnaise to the batter.

. . . .

Mix a little flour into the remains of melted chocolate in the pan to get the last bit of chocolate out of the pan.

. . . .

If adding cocoa to a cake recipe that does not call for cocoa, decrease the amount of flour by 2 tablespoons for each ¼ cup of cocoa.

· · · · ·

Use cold coffee instead of water when making a chocolate cake from a box. It gives the cake a rich, mocha flavor.

· · · · ·

Make a decorative cake form such as a heart or a star with aluminum foil. Place the form on a baking sheet, fill with batter, and bake. Be sure to spray the form generously with cooking spray before pouring in the batter.

· · · · ·

To prevent cakes from cracking while they cool, add one envelope of unflavored gelatin to the dry ingredients of any cake batter. The gelatin does not change the flavor or moistness of the cake.

· · · · ·

When substituting oil for solid shortening in a cake batter, use ⅓ less than the amount of solid shortening suggested.

To keep holes out of a cake, run a knife through the batter after mixing.

. . . . .

Fill cake pans about ⅔ full and spread batter well into the sides and corners, leaving a slight hollow in the center.

. . . . .

After adding batter to cake pans, tip slightly from side to side to level the dough.

. . . . .

To avoid broken corners or edges on cakes, grease the pan and line it with greased wax paper. After baking, invert pan and peel off the wax paper.

. . . . .

Use paper coffee filters to line 8-inch (20-centimeter) cake pans. Flatten into a large circle and lay it on the bottom of the pan.

. . . . .

Use shortening to grease the base and sides of baking tins, then dust with flour.

. . . . .

If no metal skewer is available to test a cake for doneness, use a cocktail stick or a piece of raw spaghetti.

. . . . .

A cake is done when it shrinks slightly from the sides of the pan or if it springs back when touched lightly with a finger.

. . . . .

"Look on the world as a big fruitcake; it wouldn't be complete without a few nuts in it." —Unknown

For extra moistness in all cakes, add a pan of water to the bottom oven shelf when baking.

. . . .

If a cake is a little overcooked and dry when taken from the oven, place a thick folded towel over the top of the cake until it cools to soften the texture.

. . . .

To flatten a cake with a small crown, put a plate on top of it immediately after you take it from the oven. Push the plate down gently.

. . . .

Rub a cooling rack with vegetable oil to prevent the top of cakes from sticking to it.

. . . .

Dust the serving plate with icing sugar to prevent a freshly baked cake from sticking to it.

. . . .

If a fruitcake is slightly dry, pierce randomly with a skewer and pour brandy or fruit juice over.

. . . .

If a rich fruit cake is very dry, break it up and add melted butter and a measure of brandy, leave overnight, and then press firmly into a pudding bowl. Steam for an hour and use as a dessert pudding.

. . . . .

To keep loaf cakes fresher longer, cut slices from the middle rather than from the end. When finished slicing, firmly push the two leftover sections together. Or fasten a slice of bread to the cut edge of a cake with toothpicks to keep the cake from drying out.

. . . . .

To keep a cake moist, put half an apple in the cake box.

. . . . .

When having to remove that first piece of pie or cake, the piece will slide out easier if an additional slice is cut.

. . . . .

To get more pieces from a round cake, cut a circular ring around the center of the cake, leave intact. Cut slices all around the outside ring area and then cut the inside area.

If the bottom of a cake is burnt, freeze until frozen then use a serrated knife to scrape off the burnt parts.

. . . .

To cut a fresh cake, use a wet knife. To cut a frosted cake, rinse the knife in hot water each time you cut a slice.

. . . .

Fruitcakes will keep indefinitely if buried in icing sugar and placed in a tightly sealed tin.

. . . .

If the oven door opened too soon, this sudden rush of cold air into a warm or hot oven will result in the cake collapsing and coming out flat. The oven door should not be opened until three-quarter's the way through allowed cooking time.

. . . .

The oven door being slammed shut can jolt the cake mixture, knock out or deflate all the trapped air bubbles, and will result in the cake collapsing.

. . . .

Line a cake tin with a strip of double thickness foil that's long enough to overhang both sides before storing an iced cake. It will make it easier to remove without damaging the icing.

FROSTING & FILLING

No frosting is necessary if plenty of powdered sugar is sprinkled on top of a cake before putting it into the oven.

. . . .

To cool a cake quickly for frosting, freeze the layers in the cake pans for one hour or while making the frosting, then remove them from the pans and frost them.

· · · · ·

If tiers of a multilayer cake are slipping when applying frosting, insert strands of uncooked spaghetti, skewers, or toothpicks to secure the layers of cake together. Carefully pull out the supports when the frosting has set.

· · · · ·

When frosting cakes, always anchor the bottom cake layer to the serving plate with a dab of frosting.

· · · · ·

Frosting that is too thick will tear the cake. Thin it with a few drops of water or milk.

· · · · ·

When filling and frosting a cake, place first layers with bottom side up and place last layer with the topside up.

· · · · ·

To prevent cake filling from soaking into the cake, sprinkle layers lightly with icing sugar before spreading the filling.

· · · · ·

To split a cake into layers, loop a length of waxed dental floss around the outside of the cake at the point to cut, then cross the ends and pull gently but firmly. The floss will cut right through the cake.

· · · · ·

To split layers evenly, measure halfway up the sides and insert wooden picks regularly into the cake all around. Rest a long serrated knife on the wooden picks, using them as a guide where to slice. Discard wooden picks before proceeding with the icing.

. . . .

For a fast topping for cakes, place a paper doily with a large design on top of the cake and then dust with icing sugar. Gently lift doily off the cake.

. . . .

Sift powdered sugar for frosting when using a pastry bag. Clumps in the sugar can clog a pastry tip.

. . . .

A strong plastic sandwich bag makes a good pastry bag. Spoon frosting into the bag, then snip off one corner of the bag to create the size of opening needed. Poke a tiny hole in one corner for an extra-thin writing tip.

. . . .

To easily fill an icing bag, stand an empty pastry bag in a tall drinking glass. Roll the bag's edges over the sides of the glass and fill the bag.

. . . .

Frosting will look more professional if first frosted with a thin layer and allowed to set. Then apply a second coat.

. . . .

If frosting is too thin, but it is already in the icing bag, refrigerate for an hour. It will thicken up slightly.

. . . .

Use the icing as soon as it is made. All icing sets up quickly and either forms a crust or becomes very stiff.

. . . .

Add a pinch of baking powder to homemade icing or frosting. It will help it stay moist and not crack. A little salt added to cake icings prevents them from sugaring.

. . . .

To prevent icing from running off a cake, dust the surface lightly with cornstarch before icing.

. . . .

When making lemon icing, add 2 teaspoons custard powder to every 8 ounces (225 grams) icing sugar and mix with the juice of a lemon.

. . . .

To make coffee essence for adding to sauces or icing, dissolve 1 tablespoon instant coffee in 2 teaspoons boiling water.

. . . .

For quick chocolate icing, sprinkle grated chocolate or mint chocolates over the top of the cake and place in the oven or under a medium grill for a few minutes. Spread evenly.

. . . .

Sprinkle toppings on while the icing is fresh and sticky.

. . . . .

Always let buttercream frosting warm to room temperature before thinning it down for use.

. . . . .

Thin buttercream icing with a little evaporated milk or warm water or use hot water or coffee for cold chocolate buttercream icing and mix in with an icing spatula.

. . . . .

Use a new watercolor brush to write a message on plain confectioners' sugar icing. Dip the brush in food coloring and write the message.

. . . . .

Store buttercream icing in an airtight container in the refrigerator. Fresh is best though.

. . . . .

To color and flavor icing sugar frosting, add a little unsweetened powdered drink mix (e.g., cocoa) or use smooth peanut butter.

. . . . .

For spice and carrot cake frosting, use ½ cup maple syrup instead of milk and vanilla extract.

. . . . .

Add 1 teaspoon cornstarch to fudge frosting for a smooth frosting.

. . . . .

For chocolate frosting, combine sweetened condensed milk with powdered cocoa until frosting consistency is reached.

• • • •

Obtain a sherry flavor by combining rose and almond extracts, while vanilla and almond combined gives a pistachio flavor.

• • • •

When icing a cake, dip the knife into milk to help to make the icing spread smoothly and easily on the cake.

• • • •

Press biscuit cutter shapes lightly into cake icing then fill in the outline with tinted icing in desired colors.

• • • •

To make a topping for gingerbread or coffeecake, add 1 tablespoon butter and 1 tablespoon lemon juice to 2 cups fruit syrup, heat until bubbly, and thicken with 2 tablespoons flour.

Make a cake glaze from a potato by boiling it and mixing with ⅛ cup icing sugar and a few drops of vanilla essence.

. . . . .

A clean, squeezable plastic bottle is great for decorating cakes. Just fill it with the required color, screw on the pointed tip, and get to work on the cake.

. . . . .

To freeze a frosted cake, put it in the freezer without any wrapping. Once it has frozen, wrap it and replace. This keeps the frosting from sticking to the wrapping.

. . . . .

Cakes, biscuits, and other baked goods look elegant when served on a pedestal plate. If you do not have one, create one by putting a dinner or cake plate on top of a short, wide glass or sturdy vase.

Cupcakes & Muffins

For cupcakes and small fancy cakes, grease pans well on the bottoms but little or none on sides. Fill them only half full.

. . . . .

To divide batter evenly into muffin tins, use an ice cream scoop to transfer batter from the mixing bowl.

. . . . .

When baking muffins or cupcakes in paper liners, spray liners with nonstick cooking spray and they will peel off easily.

. . . . .

"Before anything else, preparation is the key to success."
—Alexander Graham Bell

Before putting muffins or a cake into the oven, wipe off drips from the rim of the pan so they will not get baked on.

· · · · ·

When muffins or cakes are difficult to remove from the tin, place a wet towel beneath the hot pan for a minute.

· · · · ·

Use no more than 1–2 tablespoons oil or butter to 1 cup flour in muffins and quick breads.

· · · · ·

The secret to good muffins is in the lumps. Muffin batter should be gently stirred just until all the dry ingredients are moistened, resulting in a lumpy batter. The lumps will disappear during baking.

· · · · ·

Avoid using an electric mixer or stirring muffin batter vigorously. Over-stirring creates tough muffins with pointed tops. Level off the batter in muffin tins.

· · · · ·

Depending on the amount of liquid being used in a recipe, batter can range from runny to very thick. As a general rule, the thinner the batter, the lighter the muffins when baked. Thick, sloppy batter can yield moist muffins with extra keeping power.

· · · · ·

Fresh buttermilk will give muffins a special moistness and flavor. When buttermilk is used in a recipe, add ½ teaspoon baking soda per cup of buttermilk.

. . . .

For high rising, rounded tops on muffins, preheat the oven to 240°C/500°F/Gas 9. As soon as the muffins are put into the oven, decrease to the temperature stated in the recipe. Remember to decrease the baking time.

. . . .

Top muffins with a crumb topping. Combine ½ cup each of flour, brown sugar, rolled oats or muesli, 1 teaspoon cinnamon, and 2 ounces (50 grams) cold butter, cut into small pieces. Pulse in a food processor until the mixture forms fine crumbs. Sprinkle on unbaked muffins.

. . . .

Insufficient stirring or cooking at too low a temperature can cause a coarse texture in muffins. Holes in muffins, peaks in the center, and soggy texture are due to over-mixing.

. . . .

For evenly rounded tops on nut breads and muffins, grease baking pans or muffin cups on the bottom and only ½ inch (1.2 centimeters) up the sides. This allows the batter to cling to the sides of the pan instead of sliding back down.

. . . .

When making brownies, remember that adding more egg to the batter makes them lighter and more cake-like. Less egg makes them thicker and chewier.

. . . .

Brownies are cooked properly when the edges look hard, the top has cracked slightly, and the surface has a glassy appearance. The center should be firm.

. . . .

Whirl granulated sugar in a blender until powdery and roll cooked brownie squares in it for a sparkling white coating.

. . . .

Gingerbread tastes better when some fresh grated orange or lemon rind is added to the batter.

. . . .

When making gingerbread, use coffee instead of water in the batter.

. . . .

Bake cream puffs in muffin cups to prevent them from spreading.

. . . .

Soft dropping consistency is when a little of the mixture drops from the spoon by itself when the spoon is tipped. Dropping consistency is when a small amount of the mixture will fall from the spoon if gently shaken. Stiff dropping consistency is when the spoon has to be shaken more vigorously before the mixture drops.

. . . .

To stop the jam bubbling out of jam tarts before the pastry is cooked, store the jam in the refrigerator before use.

COOKIES & BARS

Cake flour is usually too tender for cookies; use all-purpose flour unless otherwise instructed.

. . . .

If substituting butter for margarine in a recipe, remember butter will make a crisper cookie while margarine makes a softer cookie.

. . . .

Use only a little flour when rolling out cookie dough as this can stop the cookies from spreading and give a hard texture. Sprinkle the board with powdered sugar instead of flour.

. . . .

Leave sticky cookie dough in the bowl for 10 minutes before adding a small amount of flour. This allows the flour to fully absorb the liquids. Mix well after each addition.

. . . .

Store cookie dough in the refrigerator in empty frozen juice cans; insert dough and tightly cover the can with foil, then chill. When ready to bake, cut the bottom off the can and use it to push out the dough as the cookies are sliced. When slicing, use the sharpest knife. Give dough a quarter turn occasionally so the bottom does not flatten.

. . . .

Keep the dough cool when making cookies. Warm dough softens the fat before cooking. This causes the cookie dough to spread more in the oven, leaving the cookies less flaky. Refrigerate the dough for an hour before baking.

. . . . .

When working cookie dough with your hands, wet the hands first to keep the dough from sticking to them.

. . . . .

Roll cookie dough, especially when it is soft and difficult to handle, between two sheets of plastic wrap or wax paper to get it as thin as required without having to use additional flour. Remove the top paper and cut cookies.

. . . . .

Cookies will be crisp on the outside and flaky in the center if the dough is rolled thin and then folded over once before cutting out cookies. They will also split open easily when ready to butter them.

. . . . .

Roll chilled cookie dough in colored or cinnamon sugar, ground nuts, or flaked coconut before slicing and baking.

When cutting out cookies, try to get as many cookies as possible from the first rolling. Too much re-rolling may cause them to become tough and dry.

. . . .

When rolling out cookie dough to cut, use a thin dusting of confectioners' sugar instead of flour on the board. The flour tends to make the dough thicker and heavier, while the dusting of sugar will help the cookies to brown evenly.

. . . .

Cookies do not have to be round. Roll the dough into a rectangle and cut out square shapes; this avoids re-rolling it.

. . . .

To keep cookie dough from sticking to cookie cutters, chill the dough thoroughly before rolling it out. Spray or dip the cookie cutter in warm salad oil before pressing into the dough and the cookies will cut cleanly.

. . . .

The sharp open end of a clean can makes a good cookie cutter. Dip the cutter in flour before using. Lift cut-outs with a long, thin spatula for less chance of distortion.

. . . .

For a quick glaze for sugar cookies, beat an egg white until just frothy and brush over the unbaked cookies. Sprinkle with sugar and bake.

. . . .

To form drop cookies, drop them onto the baking sheet and press them with the bottom of a water glass that has been dipped in sugar.

. . . .

To get cookie dough to drop without sticking, dip the spoon in milk first.

. . . .

Use a small ice cream scoop to spoon out cookie dough and make them a uniform size. It also keeps the fingers clean. If the dough is soft and difficult to work with, put the bowl in refrigerator or freezer until firm enough to shape.

. . . .

For soft-sided cookies, bake them in a pan with sides and put the cookies close together. For crisp cookies bake them on a cookie sheet with spaces between the cookies.

. . . .

Make cookies uniform in size.

. . . .

Oatmeal cookies are crunchier when the oatmeal is lightly browned in the oven then cooled before using.

. . . .

Add new flavor to ginger cookies by substituting cold coffee for the water in the recipe.

. . . .

For a beautiful glaze on cookies and cakes, mix one part softened ice cream with three parts confectioners' sugar and spread. Allow to set for 2 hours.

. . . .

Check cookies at minimum baking time.

. . . .

Cookies will not burn on the bottom if cold water is run over the base of the pan between batches. If cookies do burn, scrape away the blackened parts with a kitchen grater.

. . . .

Let cookies cool on the baking sheet for 1–2 minutes, just long enough to firm them slightly and make it easier to slide them off the sheet and onto a rack.

. . . .

Cookies stuck to the pan lift off easily if the baking sheet is returned to the oven briefly or rested on a damp tea towel.

. . . .

If you don't have enough cookie sheets while baking, spoon the remaining cookie dough onto large sheets of lightly greased aluminum foil. When a cookie sheet becomes free, cool it and lay the foil with the cookie dough on the sheet.

. . . .

When a cookie sheet is floured after greasing, cookies made from thin batters will be less likely to spread during baking.

. . . .

Always bake bars on the middle rack in the oven and cookies on the top rack. If baking more than one pan at a time, place them at different angles on different racks to allow maximum circulation of heat. Alternate their placement on the racks halfway through the baking time.

. . . . .

Let cookies cool completely before storing. Store different types of cookies in separate containers so they will keep their original flavor and texture.

. . . . .

To keep homemade cookies fresh, put a slice of white bread or crumpled tissue paper in the bottom of the container.

. . . . .

Freeze extra cookie dough in balls on a cookie sheet. When frozen, place in a freezer bag and store in the freezer. Cookie dough can be frozen up to three months in an airtight container or refrigerated 3–4 days. When a batch of cookies is needed, take out the required amount, place them on a cookie sheet, and bake in the oven.

. . . . .

When freezing cookies with a frosting, place them in the freezer unwrapped for about two hours then place in a freezer-proof, lidded box and they will not stick together.

. . . . .

To refreshen and heat cookies, put them in a dampened paper bag, twist it closed, and heat in the oven until warm.

. . . . .

Soft stale cookies that are not iced or cream-filled can be returned to former crispness by spreading them out on a baking sheet and heating in an oven at 275°F/140°C/Gas 1 for 10 minutes.

. . . .

Crush a couple of packets of plain cookies in a strong plastic bag with a rolling pin and empty into a pan with enough butter to combine them. Add any flavoring such as cocoa or peppermint, pour into a pan lined with foil, press down well, and leave in the fridge. When cold, cover with melted chocolate and cut into squares.

CHEESECAKE & CUSTARD

When making cheesecakes, the cream cheese should be thoroughly softened before starting to mix with the other ingredients. Firm cheese will not blend properly with the other ingredients and the finished product will be lumpy.

. . . .

To prevent cracks in cheesecake, after beating the cream cheese until light and fluffy, beat in the remaining ingredients just until incorporated. Beating in excess air can make the cheesecake puff dramatically in the oven then collapse toward the end of the baking period.

. . . .

Run a knife between the edge of the cheesecake and the side of the pan as soon as it is removed from the oven. This allows the cake to pull away cleanly from the sides of pan as it contracts while cooling.

. . . .

After removing a cheesecake from the oven, keep it away from draughts and cold places while it cools. Too sudden a temperature change can cause the top of the cheesecake to crack.

. . . .

To preserve the creamy texture of a frozen cheesecake, thaw it in the refrigerator for 12 hours before serving.

. . . .

Fresh egg custards are very delicate in nature and can curdle very easily. To prevent one from curdling or splitting, ensure the milk is at boiling point when adding to the egg mixture; this will drastically reduce the actual cooking time.

. . . .

Ensure the eggs are fresh. As eggs go stale, they lose their thickening properties.

. . . .

Most recipes for fresh egg custards do not contain a thickening agent but the addition of a little flour helps to stabilize the mixture and thicken it.

. . . .

As soon as the mixture thickens slightly and coats the back of the spoon, it is ready. Remove from the heat immediately and strain into a clean bowl.

. . . .

If planning to unmold a baked custard, beat the eggs only slightly before adding them to the liquid. This will keep the custard firm when baked. Too much beating produces a light, porous custard.

CHOCOLATE & CARAMEL

Choose chocolate that has a glossy, unblemished surface. A grayish color can develop on chocolate. This is called "bloom" and is an indication that the chocolate has been improperly stored and/or has melted and hardened again allowing the cocoa butter to rise to the surface. Flavor and quality will not be lessened and the grayish color or "bloom" will disappear when the chocolate is melted.

. . . .

Buy chocolate you have tasted first. To judge a good chunk of chocolate, place a piece on your tongue and hold it in your mouth allowing it to slowly melt. If it coats your mouth with a smooth, velvety feel that's a good sign you are eating an excellent and, most likely, an expensive piece of chocolate. A sandy, grainy texture however should be avoided.

. . . .

Do not store chocolate in the refrigerator or freezer because when it is brought to room temperature, condensation will form on the surface of the chocolate and affect its ability to melt smoothly. Chocolate should never be stored in or near very aromatic foods.

. . . .

"Strength is the capacity to break a chocolate bar into four pieces with your bare hands—and then eat just one of the pieces." —Judith Viorst

Keep chocolate at room temperature to prevent it from splintering and flying around when chopped; cold chocolate is difficult to cut. To chop chocolate in a food processor, chill the chocolate slightly and pulse it just until chopped.

. . . .

When melting chocolate alone, even a drop of water accidentally added could cause the chocolate mixture to "seize," meaning the chocolate will tighten and form into an unworkable mass. If this should happen, add a few drops of vegetable oil to the chocolate to allow it to relax enough that other ingredients can be mixed in.

. . . .

Chocolate chips, also known as morsels, are fine for cookie baking, but do not melt them down as they become a thick consistency and are difficult to use because they contain significantly less cocoa butter than average chocolate bars.

. . . .

The better tasting the chocolate used the better the chocolate dessert. Select chocolate that has an appetizing chocolate smell.

. . . .

Chocolate in good condition will snap cleanly when broken while poor quality chocolate will crumble.

. . . .

When melting dark or white chocolate for a glaze, chop each square into four pieces and place over hot, not boiling, water. Stir constantly until about a third is unmelted. Remove from heat and continue stirring until smooth. The chocolate should feel lukewarm. The solid chocolate will stabilize the melted portion to make it set firm and glossy.

. . . .

Take care when melting chocolate in the microwave as it can overcook and burn easily.

. . . .

To shave chocolate, carefully draw a vegetable peeler across the side of a chilled bar of chocolate.

. . . .

To blend chocolate smoothly into hot milk, melt the chocolate and stir the lukewarm mixture into the milk. Beat until smooth.

Cocoa keeps very well when stored at room temperature in the original container. It retains its freshness and quality almost indefinitely if sealed securely. Do not refrigerate.

. . . .

For a classic caramel sauce, heat 1 cup heavy cream to just below a simmer. Cook 2 cups sugar and 1 cup water in a heavy-bottomed saucepan over a medium heat, stirring occasionally, until the sugar is dissolved and the syrup clear. Continue to cook without stirring until the syrup comes to a boil, washing down the sides of the pan with a wet pastry brush to prevent crystals from forming. (Or cover the pan for a few minutes to dissolve any crystals.) Cook until liquid is a medium amber color. Remove from heat. Carefully pour in ½ cup hot cream; the mixture will sputter. When it settles down, whisk in the remaining ½ cup hot cream. Stir in a pinch salt, ½ teaspoon pure vanilla extract, and 2 tablespoons cold unsalted butter. Serve warm or cool and refrigerate until required.

. . . .

When making caramel sauce, always stir the sugar and water gently before they boil to thoroughly dissolve the sugar. Otherwise, the sugar may recrystallize into a hard lump. Gentle stirring prevents the sugar from splashing onto the pan's sides and crystallizing, making the caramel grainy. For the same reason, do not stir it after it begins boiling. Do not stick a finger into the caramel to taste it or check the color as it can cause a bad burn. Either cook in a white pot, which will show color changes clearly, or dip a strip of white cardboard into the sauce to check.

. . . .

As soon as the syrup changes color, swirl the pan to give an even hue. From this point, the process moves quickly, so watch closely. The only way to ruin caramel is to burn it.

. . . .

As soon as the syrup is a golden amber color, remove it from the heat. It will continue cooking off heat for a few seconds and turn a shade darker.

Index

Also Available

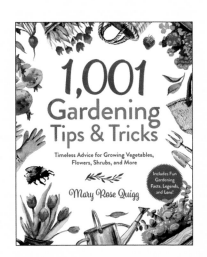

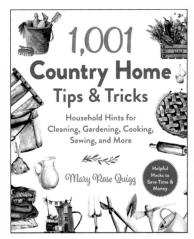

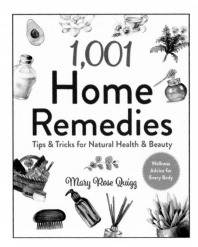